CARING FOR YOUR LAWN

Paul Pouliot

CARING FOR YOUR LAWN

HABITEX BOOKS

- Cover Design by MICHEL BERARD
- Cover photograph by W. H. PERRON & CO. LTD.
  The lawn was sown with Special Landscaper's lawn-seed mixture.
- Interior Design by MICHEL BERARD
- Illustrations by LEO BERGERON
- English language production supervision by:
  AMPERSAND PUBLISHING SERVICES INC., Toronto

 2

Exclusive Distributor:
Collier-Macmillan Canada Ltd.
539 Collier-Macmillan Drive
Cambridge, Ontario N1R 5W9
Tel. (416) 449-7115 / (519) 621-2440

ISBN-0-88912-027-7

Bibliothèque nationale du Québec
Dépôt légal — 1er trimestre 1976

I dedicate this book to the members of the Horticultural and Ecological Society of Laval.

Paul Pouliot

SOURCES

Photographs:

Agri-Tech, Inc., Boucherville, P. Qué.
Agriculture Canada, Ottawa, Ont.
Jacobsen Mfg. Co., Racine, Wisconsin, U.S.A.
Ontario Ministry of Agriculture and Food, Toronto, Ont.
Outdoor Power Equipment Institute,
  Washington, D.C., U.S.A.
W. H. Perron and Co. Ltd., Laval, P. Qué.
J. A. St-Aubin et Frère, Seedsmen,
  Saint-Léonard, P. Qué.
The Lawn Institute, Marysville, Ohio, U.S.A.
Toro Manufacturing Corp.,
  Minneapolis, Wisconsin, U.S.A.

Documentation:

Agri-Tech, Inc., Boucherville, P. Qué.
Agriculture Canada, Ottawa, Ont.
American Potash Institute, Atlanta, Georgia
Canadian Industries Ltd.
  (Lawns and Gardens Division), Montréal, Qué.
Irriga-Matic Ltd., Boucherville, P. Qué.
Jacobsen Mfg. Co., Racine, Wisconsin, U.S.A.
Laval Seeds Inc., Laval, P. Qué.
Ontario Ministry of Agriculture and Food, Toronto, Ont.
W. H. Perron and Co. Ltd., Laval, P. Qué.
Quebec Council of Vegetable Production,
  Québec, P. Qué.
Quebec Ministry of Agriculture, Québec, P. Qué.
Royal Canadian Golf Association, Montréal, P. Qué.
J. A. St-Aubin et Frère, Seedsmen,
  Saint-Léonard, P. Qué.
The Lawn Institute, Marysville, Ohio, U.S.A.
Toro Manufacturing Corp.,
  Minneapolis, Wisconsin, U.S.A.

Table of contents

Chaper VI — Mowing and Watering

Chapter VII — The Enemies of the Lawn

Chapter VIII — Tools and Equipment

Introduction

A beautiful lawn is the most important element in the
landscaping of a property. But if your property is to be really
well laid out, you need more than a lawn where the grass
is thick and luxurious and a lovely deep green. You must
also surround your house with tastefully arranged,
good-quality plants. You must be determined to have
beautiful grounds around your home. If you are not, there
is little possibility that the property will be anything
other than ordinary. Certainly, to get a lawn into first-class
condition and keep it that way demands a considerable
amount of dedication on your part and the willingness
to look after it regularly, to mow, fertilize and water
it regularly and adequately.

Furthermore, it is wasted effort to carefully plant borders,
flowerbeds, trees, and shrubs if the lawn is relegated to
second place in your landscaping plans. In short, it is
essential that you regard your lawn as the foundation —
the "background of the picture" if you like — that holds
together all the other elements of the ornamental
layout of your property — and heightens their effect.

A well-planned garden that includes a lawn consisting of
healthy, vigorous grass adds considerably to the value
of the property and also provides a welcoming atmosphere
which brings pleasure to all. However, one or two neglected
lawns in the neighbourhood will adversely affect the
appearance — and the value — of all the surrounding
properties.

It is not a difficult task to create a fine lawn and to keep

it in good condition. However, a certain basic knowledge
is essential. The object of this book is to give the
reader this essential information.

Most people who have only just taken up gardening as a
hobby usually undertake far too many garden tasks during
their first season — with the result that a good number
of them become discouraged by their lack of success.
Incidentally, gardening is much more of an art than a
science — at least as far as the amateur is concerned. This
is particularly true in the case of beginners. I would
therefore advise them to proceed one step at a time: to
acquire a minimum of experience, to follow a well thought
out programme of work and to take into account their
resources and capabilities.

If you are dealing with a new property, why not concentrate
your efforts on creating a fine lawn — a lawn consisting
of high-quality rich green grass, free of all weeds Add
some annuals, in borders, flowerbeds or containers, two
or three trees, well chosen and carefully planted, some
shrubs placed where they will produce the best possible
effect — and there you have an excellent beginning for your
landscaping. Then, after this initial success, you can try
your hand with rock gardens, hedges, perennials and hardy
summer-flowering bulbs. You might even add a patio,
and so on.

Just like a flowerbed or a kitchen-garden, a lawn requires
certain basic attention. As in the case of any garden,
the soil must be prepared for sowing. Furthermore, to
ensure normal growth, grass requires the addition of
nutritive elements, and weeds — which all too often engage
the grass in a bitter struggle for the available space,
nourishment and water — must be eliminated.

Insect pests and lawn-grass diseases must be tracked
down and controlled before they do too much damage. In
addition, lawn-grass needs water, just like trees, shrubs and
vegetables. The essential difference bettween the lawn

and the rest of the garden is that the former involves dealing with a solid mass or strong concentration of plants, rather than with individual or isolated plants, as in the case of the flowerbeds or borders. On this basis alone, the horticultural methods required in the two cases are completely different.

A good soil is the main requisite for success with a lawn. Few amateur gardeners are lucky enough to have the ideal soil — which is a good deep garden loam, well-drained, friable, rich in organic matter and well provided with nutritive elements. Most soils are lacking in organic matter and deficient in fertilizing elements — they contain too much clay or sand, and are either poorly drained or dry out too quickly.

To give my readers a basic knowledge of the physical and chemical properties of soils — knowledge which is necessary to maintain a lawn properly — I have provided, at the beginning of this book, a brief outline of the science of soils and of their physical and chemical properties. I have examined, one by one, the elements which are necessary if a soil is to yield high-quality grass. I have also dwelt at some length on drainage, since most of the problems encountered in the growing of grass are connected with that subject.

My readers will become familiar with the various kinds of lawn grasses currently available, and this knowledge will help in the choice of the most appropriate grasses for their own particular properties. For example, those who dislike mowing their lawns, or who find it hard to get lawn-grass to grow in certain areas of their property, will be glad to learn of carpeting plants which will solve their problems for them.

My readers will also learn all the various aspects of maintaining a lawn: preparing the ground, fertilizing, mowing, watering, weeding, destroying insects, recognizing diseases and preventing winter damage. I have also included

information on the various tools and equiment available
(including watering and irrigation systems).

During the preparation of this book, I have consulted the
works of many scientists specializing in various aspects of
plant production — particularly in the growing of grass:
Dr. James B. Beard of the Department of Plant Production
at the State University of Michigan, at East Lansing;
Dr. Robert W. Schery, Director of the Lawn Institute,
Marysville, Ohio; Dr. K. M. Pretty of the American Potash
Institute, Port Credit, Ontario; Dr. Jack Eggens of the
Department of Horticultural Sciences at the University of
Guelph, Ontario, and Dr. W. E. Cordukes of the Ornamental
Plant Division, the Plant Research Institute, Agricultue
Canada, Ottawa; and Dr. Houston B. Couch, Professor of
Phytopathology at the Polytechnic Institute and State
University of Virginia at Blacksburg.

Not only does a lawn offer aesthetic interest, it is also of
importance in the quality of the urban environment. It must
not be forgotten that we live in the age of ecology — the
science of interaction between living organisms and their
environment. People are becoming more and more interested
in preserving the balance between man-made structure and
Nature. In cities where pollution in all its forms is a daily
problem, lawns and all other green plants play a major role
in the improvement of the environment. Thus, patches
of greenery in urban areas provide certain advantages which
are too often unknown to the general public.

Green leaves purify the air by absorbing carbon dioxide
(CO_2) which is a major air pollutant and by liberating
oxygen. Incidentally, lawn-grasses resist atmospheric
pollution better than most other plants. It is interesting
to note that a medium-sized lawn consisting of healthy,
vigourous grass can produce enough oxygen for the daily
requirements of eight people. In common with other
ornamental plants, lawn-grasses cut down excessive heat
by means of transpiration, which can lower the temperature

of the soil by 20 degrees or more in comparison with that of a solid surface. According to recent research, the temperature 5 feet above a lawn can be as much as 10 degrees lower than that above an ungrassed surface. Furthermore, lawns and ornamental plants form a sound-insulating barrier which reflects, absorbs and deadens the noise of traffic, as well as other undesirable noises from the street and from the neighbourhood.

Paul Pouliot

Chapter 1
The Soil

To enable you to maintain your lawn properly, you need a certain minimum knowledge of the physical and chemical properties of soils. You must realize that it is the soil that provides lawn-grasses with the essential requirements: support, warmth, air, water and nutritive elements. Therefore, it is very important that those who wish to have, and to keep, a fine lawn should know something of soils and their properties, so that they may use methods of maintenance which will incorporate the latest advances in soil science, and thus achieve the highest possible quality of grass.

Here, then, is a brief résumé of certain principles and properties of soils which have a bearing on the growing of grass.

Let me begin by saying that soil science is divided into two branches: **pedology,** which deals with soil as a physical body, and which throws light on the origin, formation and distribution of soils; and **edaphology,** which concerns itself with the physical and chemical properties of soils, as well as studying their microbiology and their fertility.

PEDOLOGICAL ASPECTS

Soils are developed from an unconsolidated mass commonly known as the "mother material". This material is classified according to its origin and may include: (1) a mother rock, channelled away and broken up **in situ;** (2) organic deposits; and (3) material transported from its place of origin by water, wind, ice or simple gravity. The five principal factors which influence the formation of soil are: (1) climate (2) topography (3) the mother material (4) time and (5) organisms. Temperature and water are the major aspects of climate as far as the formation of soils is concerned.

As soils are formed, so strata or "horizons" are developed, each endowed with its own distinctive properties. A

A high-quality lawn of selected grasses is the basic element in the landscaping of a property. It enhances the plants which have been chosen to complement the architectural style of the house.

vertical cut across the various horizons is known as a "profile", and the characteristics of this profile serve as a basis for the classification of the soil.

In Canada, soils are classified and described within the framework of a programme undertaken jointly by the Federal Ministry of Agriculture and the various Provincial Ministries of Agriculture. In compiling the inventory of resources of the earth of a given sector (usually approximating the area of a county), soils are registered according to their differences in texture, drainage, topography, rock content, and their chemical and physical characteristics. Within the framework of the system of classification that has been adopted, the mother material is described, together with the arrangement of the horizons and the characteristics of the soil; the result is known as a "soil series". A soil series is subdivided into "types" of soil, according to texture, whether the stratum is sandy or clayey, and so on. Variations within a given type of soil are known as "phases", and are characterized by factors such as angle of inclination, erosion, rock-content and depth. Data provided by these soil studies (both written reports and maps) can be of great assistance in the maintenance of lawns. Besides describing the location and extent of various types of soil, the reports give useful information, such as their adaptability to a given method of cultivation, depth, general state of fertility, drainage, and hydrographic details.

PHYSICAL PROPERTIES OF SOILS

The physical properties of soils depend on various determining factors such as the temperature and humidity of the surrounding atmosphere, and their chemical and micro-biological properties. Therefore, physical properties are important in the determination of the productivity of the particular soil under consideration.

Texture

The texture of a soil is a function of the size and nature of the particles that make up that soil. Mineral particles less than 2 mm in size are divided according to size into 4 separate soils or categories of soil as follows: coarse sand = 2 to 0.2 mm; fine sand = 0.2 to 0.02 mm; silt = 0.02 to 0.002 mm; and clay = less than 0.002 mm. * The proportions of sand, silt and clay determine the class of a soil's texture; the quantities are evaluated by analysis of the size of the particles. Once the quantities of sand, silt and clay have been established, the class of the soil's texture may be determined by "the triangle of texture" method. The separate components of soils differ in their surface area, and many physical and chemical reactions are influenced by that fact. Clayey particles have the greatest surface

---

* Source: International Society of Soil Science.

area, and this makes them important agglomerating agents in the process of soil formation. The clayey particle is also the seat of most of the chemical reactions, such as absorption. The sandy particles — which are the largest individual elements — facilitate aeration and the flow of water; while the silt particles, which, in size, lie between the sandy and the clayey particles, behave somewhat like a mixture of the two.

Agglomeration

The agglomeration of soils is defined as the grouping together of particles of soil, with the result that larger particles are formed; these are known as secondary or "agglomerated" particles. This phenomenon is of the greatest importance in soils with a high content of silt and clay. As long as the particles maintain their separate identity, the soil contains a great number of minute pores, and

It is useless to think that you will ever have a perfect lawn if the underlying base — the soil — is unsuitable for lawn-grasses. Furthermore, a regular supply of nutritive elements is essential.

is compact. In contrast, when the tiny particles agglomerate, a greater porosity is achieved, thus improving the aeration factor and the flow of water. The following factors also play important parts in the agglomeration of soils: plant roots, frost followed by thaw, watering and drying-out, and micro-biological activity.

The structure of the soil depends on the arrangement of its component particles, including agglomerated particles. Generally speaking, soils are divided into four categories according to their type of structure: prismatic, cubical, platyform and spheroidal. A soil in which no agglomeration can be detected is called a structureless soil. An example of such a soil is a very sandy soil in which the particles are all separate independent grains. The stability of the agglomerates is an important factor which may decide whether or not a soil possesses good physical properties. Stable agglomerates do not break up, and are not destroyed by watering or by tilling of the soil. In contrast, unstable agglomerates break up when watered, either because of the action of the drops of water, or because of the swelling of the particles themselves.

Porosity

The density of the soil and its porous surface are the principal characteristics which enable the general physical conditions of a soil to be defined. The density is the weight of the soil per unit of volume, and is usually expressed in grams per cubic centimeter: it may vary from 1 for a well-agglomerated soil to almost 2 for a compact soil. Organic matter contained in the soil reduces its density. Differences in the porosity of various soils are usually related to variations in density: the lower the density, the higher the porosity. The arrangement of the pores, relative to their dimensions, is a more important factor than the overall porosity. Movement of air and water within the soil takes place through the larger pores, while the smaller pores serve to maintain the moistness of the soil. The extent of porosity to air is used to denote those pores through which air is taken in at a rate comparable with the maximum rate necessitated by environmental conditions. A good soil may be divided by volume as follows: 50% solid matter, and 50% porous area. The volume of air and water in the soil should be almost equal — i.e., each of these elements should amount to approximately one quarter of the total volume. When the porous area exceeds the norm of 50%, the water flows so rapidly that the soil dries out — thus necessitating frequent watering.

Soil and air

The quantity of air within the soil depends chiefly on the porosity of the soil. This quantity is characterized by measurement of the concentrations of oxygen and carbon dioxide present, by the rate of gaseous diffusion, and by the porosity factor relative to air. Since the roots of the grass-plants breathe, they absorb oxygen and emit carbon dioxide. In the same way, the micro-organic matter in the soil absorbs oxygen and emits carbon dioxide. Thus, the quantity of air present in the soil depends on the volume of air taken in by the soil, and on the exchange of air between the soil and the atmosphere. The air found in a soil depends also on factors such as the temperature of the soil, the barometric pressure, the action of wind, and precipitation. Even though grass is better able to withstand poor aeration than other growing organisms, its roots still need oxygen. When water replaces air in the soil, the growth of the roots is restricted, and the bacterial activity within the soil is slowed down considerably. Shallow-rooted grass is unable to make full use of the available moisture and nutritive materials. The grass weakens, and becomes more susceptible to damage, disease, insects and the onslaughts of weeds.

A good soil is the main requisite for success in a lawn. High-quality grasses alone will not guarantee a fine lawn. It is of equal importance that they be planted in a suitable soil where they can take root firmly and find the nutritive elements necessary for their normal growth.

Soil and water

The water within the soil is retained in the pores by the forces of attraction between the molecules of water and the surface of the solid particles. When the water-content is low, it forms a thin layer on the surface of the particles. When this layer is very thin, the molecules of water, being very close to the surface of the particles, are pressed

27

tightly against that surface. The energy required to "capture" a given quantity of water is called the absorptive capacity of the soil — i.e., its power of sucking in moisture. When all the pores within the soil are filled with water, the soil is said to be "saturated". The water runs out of the larger pores under gravity and when the grass needs water it first takes the water stored in the medium-sized pores and finally the water from the smaller pores. The water within a soil is a function of the physical nature of that soil, and depends on three factors: (1) the surface layer, which controls absorption and infiltration; (2) the zone lying around and immediately beneath the grass roots; and (3) the zone lying well beneath the grass roots, which acts as a reservoir to replenish the upper zone as water is removed upwards from that zone. In most cases, the growth of the grass serves to protect the granules lying on the surface of the soil and also helps to produce a porous structure which facilitates the infiltration of water. Mulching forms a layer that hinders the free entry of water. Also, movement on moist soil will compress the granules on the surface and destroy their structure, thus reducing their porous surface — and this may result in an inadequate infiltration of water.

Flow of water in the soil

Once the water has penetrated the surface of the soil, it is transmitted elsewhere by a flow which may be saturated or unsaturated. If the soil is saturated, the water moves chiefly through the larger pores, under the force of gravity. Most of the time, movement of water takes place when the pores are not already filled with water — i.e., the flow is unsaturated. Basically, what is occurring is the movement of a layer of water, and the rate of movement depends chiefly on the thickness of that layer and of the layer of medium-sized pores. The water is moving from a moist soil to a drier soil; or from a zone where the water-layer is thicker to one where it is thinner. Resistance to the flow of water in the soil is a function not only of the thickness of the water-layer, but also of the continuity of that layer. In fine-textured soils, the water-layer is normally in close contact with the individual particles which enclose it, and the flow between the two is in no way restricted. In coarse-grained soils, there are fewer points of contact between the particles of soil and the adjacent water-layer and this factor may reduce the rate of flow. The flow of water through a large orifice such as a drain-pipe is comparable to that of water flowing freely in the lower layers of a very highly porous soil. Such a flow occurs only when the soil surrounding the zone of flow has become saturated. (This is the reason why a drain-pipe should be located well below the root zone.)

It is important to give the subsoil proper consideration, for it may be that the structure of the subsoil will prevent the water from flowing through it rapidly enough — with the result that the water will "back up" into the root zone and thus cause poor aeration there. When water moves out of the subsoil rather slowly you would be well advised to water or spray your lawn lightly several times a week during hot, dry spells, in order to keep the root zone moist (rather than saturated), and thus prevent damage to the grass. Generally speaking, the quantity of water in the soil can be controlled by various methods such as irrigation, drainage, proper preparation of the soil and so forth.

CHEMICAL PROPERTIES OF SOILS

Soil colloids and cation exchange

Just like the physical properties, the chemical properties of a soil are chiefly a function of the volume and type of clay and humus in that soil. Clay and humus are the materials which make up the colloidal part of the soil (the diameter of their particles is less than 1 micron). The clayey part of the soil is nearly always a mixture of the various mineral constituents of clay: its make-up can vary considerably, and will depend chiefly on the construction of the mother material. Humus is the more or less stable portion of organic matter which remains in the soil after most of the residual organic products have decomposed. It may be found alone, or with other organic colloids. Soil colloids carry excess negative charges, and act as negatively-charged ions (or 'anions') when reactions take place in the soil. The principal cations (positively-charged ions) retained by soil colloids are: Ca_2+, Mg_2+, $K+$, $Na+$, NH_4+, $H+$ and Al_3+. "Cation exchange" is the exchange that takes place between a cation in solution and another cation retained by a soil colloid. The capacity for exchange between cations is a function of the numbers and types of colloids present in the soil. Generally speaking, the more clayey or organic matter there is in a soil, the greater the capacity for cation exchange becomes. Soils with a high cation-exchange capacity are more fertile than those with a poor exchange capacity.

When cations are added to a coarse-grained soil, they are very easily washed away, since the exchange capacity of the soil is too feeble to retain them. The clayey portion of the soil can effect exchange of anions. The most common inorganic anions that can be exchanged are: $OH-$, $Cl-$, NO_3-, SO_4- and H_2PO_4-.

Reaction of the soil

The reaction of the soil refers to its acid or alkaline character. This is expressed in terms of 'pH', which measures the activity of hydrogen ions in solution. pH values run from 0 to 14: 7 represents a neutral condition, while numbers below 7 represent acidity, and numbers above 7 represent alkalinity. A soil pH between 6 and 7 is considered to be the best for growing grass, chiefly because of the availability of nutritive materials and microbic activity — since decomposition, fixation of nitrogen and nitrification are encouraged by a pH value slightly under 7. Bacterial and actinomycetal activity is reduced if the soil pH is too low. Similarly, the rate of release of nitrogen from inorganic materials and fertilizers is also restricted by too low a pH value. It is generally considered that a pH of 6.5 is the most desirable figure as far as the overall availability of nutritive materials is concerned. An acid soil is less fertile than one that has been well limed; the former contains less calcium, magnesium and phosphorus. In addition, an increase in the acidity of the soil reduces the amount of molybdenum. The solubility of manganese and aluminum is increased, and these metals may be released in quantities that are toxic to grass-plants. Over-acid soil is one of the causes of poor development of grass roots. In such conditions, the roots are only shallow, restricted in their movements and brown in colour, and the rootlets though which they draw their nourishment are either few in number or completely absent. If your soil is acid in character, as shown by a low pH value,

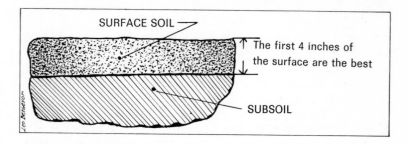

SURFACE SOIL

The first 4 inches of the surface are the best

SUBSOIL

Soil consists of two parts: the surface soil, which contains organic matter and nutritive elements for plants; and the subsoil, which lies immediately beneath the surface soil. If your surface soil is 4 inches (10 cm) or more in thickness, you are lucky. If you have only 2 or 3 inches (5 to 7.5 cm), you would be well advised to add more. Alternatively, you could improve the condition of your subsoil by adding organic matter and chemical fertilizer. The subsoil contains little or no nutritive material for plants. Generally speaking, urban plots contain a mixture of surface soil and subsoil.

the addition of lime will bring it to a neutral condition. Limestone is the material most frequently used for ths purpose and may be in the form of calcite or dolomite, or a mixture of the two. Two important considerations to bear in mind concerning the effectiveness of limestone as an agent for reducing the acidity of the soil are (1) the chemical purity of the material and (2) the size of its particles.

An alkaline soil, with a high pH value, reduces the available copper and zinc. Iron, aluminum and manganese are less soluble in an alkaline environment. Substances that may be used to increase the acidity of the soil are: elemental sulphur, sulphuric acid, aluminum sulphate and iron sulphate. The acidity of the soil may also be increased with the aid of an acidifying nitrogen fertilizer such as ammonium nitrate, ammonium sulphate, ammonium phosphate, urea, ureic substances, and certain organic substances. However, certain sources of nitrate — e.g., potassium nitrate and calcium nitrate — **decrease** the acidity of the soil.

Essential elements affecting the nourishment of grass-plants

A fertile soil should be able to produce good-quality grass. To ensure this, it must contain all the essential elements in sufficient quantity to enable it to meet the needs of the growing grass.

The essential elements, carbon (C), hydrogen (H) and oxygen (O) are usually considered separately. The reason for this is perhaps that the soil obtains these elements from the air around it, rather than from the addition of chemical fertilizers. This leaves 16 elements to be considered: nitrogen (N), phosphorus (P), potassium (K), calcium (Ca), magnesium (Mg), sulphur (S), iron (Fe), manganese (Mn), copper (Cu), zinc (Zn), boron (B) and molybdenum (Mo), as well as some sodium (Na), some chlorine (Cl), some silicon (Si) and some vanadium (V). (These last four elements have recently been shown to be beneficial to certain plants in certain special circumstances.)

Nitrogen is **the** important element in grass-growing — it is the major factor responsible for the colour and the vegetal growth of the grass. Nitrogen compounds make up 40 to 50% of the dry matter contained in protoplasm, the living, self-reproducing substance in the cells of plants. Certain nitrogen compounds migrate within the plants, moving from zones of aging to zones of growth. Since grass remains in a permanently vegetative condition, its annual requirement of nitrogen is higher than that of most plants.

Phosphorus contrbutes directly to many of the vital process of growth, and it is one of the components of the vital parts of all living cells. One of the essential roles of phosphorus compounds is to store energy and release it during certain reactions. Furthermore, phosphorus acts as a "buffer" when it comes to maintaining the pH of cells at the desired level. It plays the same role during the germination of seeds, growth of plants, maturing of seeds and development of roots and fruits. Soils with a high silt and clay content contain more phosphorus than sandy soils. Since phosphorus is easily and quickly fixed in the soil, it is not easily washed away by draining water.

Despite numerous studies, the specific role played by **potassium** in grass-plants is not fully understood. It is found in fair quantities in all parts of the plants, especially in the blades and in the growth-zones. It seems that it may be present in mobile, soluble form. The experts believe that potassium plays a part in the synthesis of proteins and carbohydrates, and that it also has something to do with the relationship that exists between water and grass. Furthermore, it is believed to help in photosynthesis, and even in winter survival, resistance to diseases and the general sturdiness of the grass.

Calcium and **magnesium** are needed in the essential growth process of grass and it is almost certain that these two elements will be lacking in highly acid soils. It does not seem that calcium is able to move freely from zones of aging to zones of growth, even though the major part of this element is soluble within the plants. Therefore the symptoms of lack of calcium are first noticeable in young tissue. Magnesium is associated with the diastatic systems, during the metabolism of phosphorus. It moves easily enough within the plants, thus the symptoms of lack of magnesium are first noticeable in the older leaves. **Sulphur** forms part of several of the products resulting from the synthesis of proteins. Generally speaking, it is found in sufficient quantity in heavy soil, but it may be lacking in a poor, sandy soil, or in a soil rich in lime.

Trace elements

Even though **iron** is not found in the structure of chlorophyll, it is an essential element in the synthesis of this substance. It acts somewhat like a catalyst in oxidation systems, and during the reduction of nitrite into nitrates within plants. Just like iron, **copper** is an essential factor in several diastatic systems associated with the process of oxidation — or, more accurately, with de-oxidization reactions. **Manganese** and iron are intimately involved in the nutrition of the grass-plants — too much of one of these elements may result in a deficiency of the other element. **Zinc** is present in all the diastatic systems of the plants. **Boron** seems to be an essential factor in the movement of sugars, and it may also play a part in the relationships of water within the cells, the solubility of calcium, and the metabolism of proteins. **Molybdenum** has been shown to be an essential element in the system of reduction of nitrates within grass-plants.

When any nutritive element is available in excessive quantities, it may influence the availability of other elements. Chloroses due to chalk have been noted on lawns of bent grass planted in soils with a high pH value. In most cases, they may be rectified by the addition of powdered ferrous sulphate or chelated (or "fixed") iron. Deficiency in iron is also aggravated by a high phosphorus content. Excessive quantities of calcium carbonate, or magnesium, or both, can bring on chlorosis. Excessive quantities of other metallic elements, including chrome, copper, zinc, cobalt, nickel and cadmium, can cause symptoms identical with those of iron deficiency.

DRAINAGE

It is impossible to create a fine lawn of healthy grass without good drainage. Nearly all the problems encountered with lawns are related to this subject.

Effect on the growth of grass

Proper drainage creates conditions favourable to the growth and development of plants and organisms living in the soil. It permits the formation of good granulation, and reduces the negative effects caused by excessive circulation of water and packing of the soil. Even in winter, when the grass is semi-dormant, drainage plays an important part in reducing the harmful effects of successive freezing and thawing of the soil. In northern areas good surface drainage can prevent the destruction of grass which occurs when water and ice build up in the immediate vicinity of the crown of the grass-plants. By lowering the level of the water-table, the formation of deep, active roots is also encouraged.

Depending on their composition, soils either retain moisture or facilitate the passage of water in various degrees. Each of them is characterized by the relative quantities of sand, silt and clay in their make-up. Organic matter — although it may be present only in minute proportions — will have a marked effect on the physical and chemical properties of soils. The movement of water and the retention of moisture depend essentially on the dimensions of the soil pores, and not on their total volume.

There are two types of pore: the large, which are known as "macropores", and the small, or "micropores". In a macropore, the water is subjected to the effects of its own weight; in a micropore, it is held with such force that it is able to move upwards by capillary attraction.

A sandy soil consists chiefly of macropores and is naturally dry. Clayey soils contain mostly micropores and tend to be moist. In a good granular silt, offering optimum conditions for grass-plants, pores should form 50% of the volume — half of these should be water-retaining micropores and the other half macropores full of air.

The old dictum: "In spring-time, a moist soil is a cold soil" is quite true as far as grass is concerned. If the soil is to warm up nicely and quickly in the spring, good drainage is necessary.

Generally speaking, at least half the pores of a well-drained soil are full of air — and here we are talking of the macropores which give the soil its texture and entrap sufficient quantities of oxygen. However, in powdery soils, the pores containing air may prove to be less than half the total number of pores, and many of them may be micropores, which will retain any mosisture in the soil. The air retained in these soils will tend to have too low an oxygen-content to provide the grass roots with the quantity of this element needed for the metabolism of the plant. In such conditions, the absorption of nutritive elements is slowed down, even when these elements are present in sufficient quantity, and the activity of the aerobic bacteria is noticeably affected. When water fails to move freely across the subsoil, an excessive accumulation of soluble salts may build up in the root zone.

The most visible effect of inadequate drainage and insufficient circulation of air in the soil is the lowering of the oxygen-content of the organic matter. This seems to result more from a lack of oxygen than from an excessive accumulation of carbon dioxide. The slowing-up of decomposition of organic residues in marshy areas is an extreme example of the retarding effect that the lack of oxygen has on the process of decomposition. No aerobic organism can function properly without oxigen. This concerns the organisms — both symbiotic and non-symbiotic — that "fix" nitrogen in the soil. Aerobic bacteria are capable of functioning in these conditions by using oxygen in compound form — they produce certain forms of iron and manganese by a process of reduction, but these forms are phytotoxic.

Grass that has been saturated by heavy rain and then exaposed to a hot sun will in many cases wilt badly within a short period of time. This "moist wilting" is aggravated by inadequate drainage. It is caused by a slow-down in the absorption of water, due to the lack of air caused by the saturation of the soil in the root zone. When the process of transpiration is stepped up under the effect of the sunlight, the loss of water coupled with the slower rate of absorption causes the plant to dry out.

The lack of aeration and adequate drainage restricts the absorption of water for several reasons: metabolism has been slowed down, and as a direct conquence of this so, too, has the absorption of water and nutritive elements. Furthermore, the lack of circulation of gases in the soil can lead to an accumulation of CO_2, which seems to increase the viscosity of the protoplasm and reduce the permeability of the plant-cells — and this also restricts the absorption of water.

Efficient drainage of the soil is essential for a good lawn, since grass-plants cannot survive in a badly-drained soil. As is well known, these plants — just like all plants — take in oxygen as they breathe and give out carbon dioxide (CO_2). To reach the roots, this oxygen must be able to penetrate the soil. Similarly, the carbon dioxide must be able to escape by passing through the space in the soil.

In a badly-drained soil — after a heavy rain, for example — water fills up these spaces in the soil, and stays there for some considerable time. The movement of air and CO_2 within the soil is slowed down as a result and this deprives the plants — in this case, the grass-plants of the lawn — of the oxygen which they simply must have for their normal growth, and also hinders the elimination of carbon dioxide.

Close-packed soil

The same situation can arise if the soil is too close-packed, or the spaces in it are too small. Poor drainage is often caused by a layer of hard, impermeable earth in the subsoil. To check the drainage of any piece of property, dig a hole two or three feet deep and fill it with water. If the level of the water has barely gone down at all after six hours, you may safety conclude that the drainage is inadequate. If the water can get through the thin layer of clayey soil that lies only a few inches beneath the top layer of your surface soil, the drainage of the land will be much improved. This underlying layer of hard material may be dug up and replaced with good soil. If this is done, it is a good idea to spread a layer of sand or gravel at the bottom of the excavation — this will facilitate the elimination of excess water.

Drainage systems

Runs of drain-pipe may also be used under the ground. These pipes, either earthenware or plastic, are usually 4 inches (10 cm) in diameter, and are installed at intervals of 25 feet (7.6 m).

With such a system, a suitable spot must be prepared beforehand to receive the surplus water which will be drained from the land. The drain-pipes should be buried 18 to 24 inches (45 to 60 cm) deep, according to the type of soil. Their slope — which is normally 4 inches in 100 feet (10 cm in 30.5 m), and never less than 2 inches in 100 feet (5 cm in 30.5 m) — will depend on the nature of the outfall, and on the total length of piping. The surface of the ground should be graded to give it a slight slope, which will help the rapid removal of surplus water. This removal of surface water will do away with the formation of pockets in the soil, and low spots on the surface.

The addition of organic matter (in the form of manure, compost, etc.) to a rich garden loam or a clayey soil improves the drainage. Organic matter, which is often described as "the life of the soil", helps the fine particles in the soil to adhere to the larger particles — with the result that spaces in the soil are enlarged. Organic matter also helps soils to absorb and retain moisture, prevents them from drying out, and helps to keep the nutritive elements from being washed away.

Chalk and garden peat

Chalk can also lighten heavy — i.e., clayey — soils. As an example, use about 80 lbs (35 kg) of ground chalk per 1000 sq ft (92 m^2) of ground, mixed into the first six inches (15 cm) of surface soil. This addition of chalk is usually carried out in the autum.

Garden peat is the most effective form of organic matter for improving light — i.e., sandy — soils, and also for lightening heavy soils. Spread the peat about 3 inches (7.5 cm) deep, and work it thoroughly into the first 8 inches (20 cm) of the soil.

Farm manure is also a marvellous source of organic matter, but it is very difficult to obtain in sufficient quantities. Gardening centres sell dried manure, which may be used to enrich a soil with organic matter. Dead leaves are another method of providing organic matter; here, the best results are obtained when the leaves are partially decomposed. Leaves which are not decomposed are difficult to mix into the soil and they can hinder the movement of water within the soil.

Nowadays more and more amateur gardeners are using a roller, grinder or pulverizer to break up their dead leaves and other organic residues in order to make compost, either for use as a mulch or for burying in the ground. Many types of this kind of equipment are available, at prices to suit all pockets. Incidentally, in certain regions garden lovers have clubbed together to buy this equipment as communal property — it is truly indispensable for anyone who wants to garden seriously.

Research has shown that compacting of the soil is **not** eliminated by the simple act of digging it up, or perforating it to improve aeration and the circulation of water. In fact, after two or three rains, the soil very often reverts to its previous condition. Improvement is effected by the admixture of organic matter.

ANALYSIS OF THE SOIL

A lawn may become greener with the aid of a little chemistry. More than for other plants in the garden, success in creating a fine lawn has a direct relationship with the chemistry of the soil.

The best way of finding out what a lawn needs is to analyze the soil. Furthermore, this may be done by any gardener with the aid of a kit available at any gardening centre. Alternatively, a sample of the soil may be sent to an analytical laboratory. Analysis of the soil indicates several things; firstly, it tells the acidity of the soil, that is, the PH; next, it shows the available quantities of nutritive elements; and finally, it determines the amount of organic matter contained in the soil.

A soil analysis report should also indicate the amount of chalk that should be added to the soil, in ground form, to neutralize its acidity; what additional quantities of phosphorus and potassium are needed to bring them up to an adequate level for lawn-grasses; how much organic matter should be added to produce some of the nitrate and retain the moisture needed by healthy grass; and also what sort of fertilizer should be added, and how often, to maintain the normal level of fertilizing elements.

Acidity of the soil

The most important factor in a soil's condition is its acidity. If the soil is too acid, plants will not grow in it. If it is not acid enough, some plants will not grow properly. Furthermore, excess acidity reduces the availability of phosphorus and other nutritional elements to the plants.

Acidity of the soil is caused by minerals such as aluminum and manganese, which combine with the phosphorus and the potassium. The calcium contained in chalk frees the phosphorus, potassium and other elements necessary for the growth of the grass-plants.

Research has established that iron also combines with phosphorus when the pH is low. Conversely, in alkaline soils, it is the phosphorus that retains the iron. In either event, these two elements are no longer available, and this causes chlorosis or anaemia in the grass-plants and reduces the levels of iron and phosphorus.

Nearly all soils contain chalk, in varying quantities and forms, and in various different compounds. Up to a certain point, this chalk content determines whether a particular soil is classed as acid or alkaline. The scale of measurement for this classification is known as the pH of a soil: it runs from 1 to 14, with 7 indicating a neutral soil — i.e., one that is neither acid nor alkaline. As is well known, soil is a living entity subject to continual change. Accordingly, chalk has a tendency to disappear from the soil in certain conditions, thus altering its pH. As an example, rain can remove from 200 to 400 lb of chalk from the soil, depending on the season.

Once they are put under cultivation to any significant degree, all soils — with a few rare exceptions — have a tendency to turn acid. Water trickling through the soil leaches out a good quantity of chalk. Another factor, which is true for all soils, is that the decomposition of organic matter produces acids. Incidentally, rainwater itself also contains acids.

Thus all soils have a natural tendency to become acid as time goes by. In the simplest terms, the acidification of a soil is the replacement, on the soil particles, of those chemical elements which are nutritious to plants, by hydrogen originating from the acids in the soil and developed by the decomposition of organic matter, or brought there by rainwater. As a soil becomes more acid, it becomes less fertile and less productive.

Should an attempt be made to increase the fertility of such a soil by the admixture of more organic matter or the spreading of more fertilizer, hardly any change will be noticeable, for both these operations will increase the acidity of the soil still further and its pH will continue to drop.

The role of chalk

Chalk neutralizes the acidity of the soil by providing it with calcium and manganese, two elements of importance in the growth of plants. By correcting the acidity of the soil, chalk reduces the toxicity of elements such as aluminum or manganese, which are more soluble in acid soils. Chalk develops a favourable environment for the multiplication of the soil's micro-organisms, and for their work, thereby facilitating the decomposition of vegetable debris; at the same time, it improves the growth of roots — especially those which absorb nutritive elements from the soil.

Chalk will help to prevent the fixation of phosphorus for which aluminum, iron and manganese are responsible in acid soils. The more acid the soil, the more phosphorus is needed to satisfy the requirements of the plants. The nutritive elements in the soil are most easily liberated at pH values between 6.0 and 7.0. The addition of chalk will not only improve the structure of the soil but will also increase the effectiveness of chemical fertilizers by increasing the availability of the elements they contain.

Chalk and chemical fertilizers

It is rarely economical to apply fertilizers containing phosphate to over-acid soils, where the tendency is for 80% to 90% of the phosphorus to be fixed chemically by iron, aluminum and manganese. Once fixed, the phosphorus is no longer available for the plants, unless the pH of the soil is improved.

Furthermore, by stimulating the decomposition of organic matter, chalk will also facilitate the liberation of nitrogen. It should be noted that nitrogen contained in a fertilizer in nitrate or protein form must be converted to nitric form by the soil bacteria before it can be used by the plant roots. For maximum efficiency of action, these bacteria require a pH in the neighbourhood of 7.0.

It might almost be said that the application of chalk improves all the good things that the soil can offer, and cuts down the effect of the bad things. The addition of chalk causes a greater liberation of phosphorus in the soil, and of potassium, magnesium, nitrogen and molybdenum — all of which are thus more beneficial to the grass-plants. At the same time, the solubility of aluminum, manganese and iron will have been reduced, and these elements will no longer have the negative effects on the growth of plants that were noticeable before. An application of chalk to an acid soil greatly increases the capacity of the plants to use any phosphates spread on the soil.

The value of chalk

The value of chalk is measured by its capacity to neutralize acids and by the fineness of its texture after grinding. The richer the chalk is in calcium (in the form of calcium carbonate), the better it is. Further, it must be borne in mind that the dissolution of the chalk is caused by the acidity of the soil. The more acid the soil, the more quickly the chalk dissolves; as the acidity drops, so the chalk dissolves more and more slowly. However, this acidity works only on the surface of the chalk particles. This is where the fineness of the grind comes into play. The finer the particles, the more surface there will be exposed to the action of the acid, and the quicker the chalk will take effect. For example, a cube of chalk with 1-inch (2.5 cm) sides will have a total surface area of 6 sq in (38.7 cm²). If this same cube is finely ground, it can offer a surface area of up to 600 sq in (3870 cm²). To complete the picture, let me just add that the fineness of the grind does not affect the solubility of the chalk in any way, it merely increases the available surface area. It is easy to see the importance of both of these factors — capacity of neutralization and fineness of grind — when judging the quality of an agricultural chalk.

Plants and their pH

The importance of a plant's pH cannot be overstressed. It must never be forgotten that every plant has its own particular, and precise, pH requirements. Thus, the moment the pH of a plant varies from the desirable figure for that plant, the plant's development will be restricted, as will its resistance, and yield. This deterioration will continue until the pH has been corrected and brought back to the proper value for that plant. Different plants and other growths do not necessarily all thrive well at the same pH.

Each plant requires an exact pH. This means that if the pH of the soil is not the correct one for a given plant, this plant will not give the yield to be expected as a result of the other attentions lavished on it. If one knows the correct pH for a plant, one can then take steps to maintain that pH value in the soil, on the one hand; and work out cultivation programmes, on the other hand, in which plants with similar pH requirements can be rotated.

The structure of a soil can give an indication as to the quantity of chalk that should be added to it. Coarse, sandy soils need less chalk to raise their pH than fine-particled soils which are often lacking in organic matter. If a soil has a floury or talcy look to it, it may be assumed that there is little organic matter in it.

FERTILIZATION

Among the essential qualities of a good grass are colour, uniform density, sufficient growth to ward off the invasions of weeds, rapid recovery from the effects of stress and absence of diseases. The two most important factors which decide the quality of the grass are plant-management and climate. These cannot really be considered separately, since the one has a strong influence on the other.

Since the sun and the weather cannot be controlled in any way, maintenance of quality depends chiefly on the adaptation of nutritional programmes to suit the dominant climate, the species of grass, the humidity pattern and the soil conditions. This is particularly difficult in areas such as Eastern Canada, where varied stress conditions may be encountered, ranging from the dryness experienced during long, hot, humid spells, through the burial under the ice and the drying-out during the winter months, to the late frosts of the spring. Every lawn has to struggle for survival. The proper management of grass, including the appropriate fertilizing, consists of setting up particular programmes geared to precise needs.

It would be impossible here to give a detailed programme of balanced nutrition, in view of the wide differences of soil and climate across Canada. In fact, there could never be one single programme of balanced nutrition, since what is adequate for certain lawn-grasses or for certain soils may well prove to be completely inapplicable in other cases.

However, it is possible to consider some of the basic principles of balanced nutrition as they relate to the production of a high-quality grass under various conditions in different parts of the country.

Balance of nutritive elements in the soil

It is essential to know the type of soil, and what nutritive elements it contains, in order to work out a rational programme for fertilizing grass.

The objects of such a programme are, first, to achieve results which will reach the target level suggested by the soil analyses, by means of corrective applications of fertilizer and, second, to maintain this level of results by applications to balance losses caused by grass clippings, leaching by water or fixation of fertilizing elements.

Although many soils in Canada are poor in phosphorus in their natural state, it is possible to obtain significant increases in phosphorus by dint of continued and well-organized applications of relatively large quantities of phosphorus on grassed surfaces. In many areas of Quebec, for example, (where the process is helped by the absence of any significant movement of phosphorus in the soil), this has been confirmed by soil analyses. Newly-laid soil surfaces are usually the poorest in available phosphorus.

The acidity or alkalinity of the soil presents few problems relative to the quality of the grass. It is known, however, that the best texture and the highest degree of uniformity are associated with a low pH; while the vigour, colour and density of grass are at their best on alkaline surfaces.

The level of nitrogen in the soil has relatively little effect on the need for fertilizing. This need is more directly connected with climatic factors and other considerations of plant-management. Leaching of nitrogen in coarse-grained soils, particularly those which are subjected to intense irrigation, increases the need for fertilizer and alters the existing balance. In a recent comparison of water-soluble nitrogen sources with sources slow to act on coarse-grained soils, researchers found significant differences in the rates of filtration as measured by the accumulation of nitrates at different levels of the profile. It was established that with water-soluble nitrogen sources, leaching took place unexpectedly soon after the spring application of the fertilizer. On the other hand, when slow-acting fertilizers were used, no noticeable increase in the amount of nitrate in the soil was established before the end of the summer. As a result of this research, it is now suggested that if water-soluble nitrogen is used on coarse-textured soils, the applications should be made more frequently. Also, over-enthusiastic irrigation should be avoided.

Although certain soils may be so poor as to require the addition of some secondary elements and trace elements over a period of several years, soils deficient in these fertilizing elements are becoming more wide-spread. This may be due to increasingly intensive soil-management programmes which tend to exhaust the soil, or to the use of more concentrated and more refined fertilizers.

Some of the differences noticed with various sources of fertilizing elements may also be caused by the reaction of secondary elements. For example, the greater yield from potassium sulphate in certain areas, as compared with potassium chlorate, may be due to the sulphur content of the former material.

Research has established that the application of sulphur to certain types of "cool-weather" grass, grown on certain soils, will improve their growth, colour and density, and will lessen the incidence of snow-mould and encroachment by annual bluegrass. The sulphur content is believed to be the reason for the superior yield from ammonium sulphate used for promoting bushier growth, better colour and a longer growth-period in lawns of fescue, bent grass and bluegrass.

Sulpher seems to do better than other nitrogen sources used for the same purposes.

This is not the place to go into further detail on the balance of fertilizing elements in the soil. However, I cannot stress too strongly the importance of maintaining continued control over the soil, since significant changes can take place in a very short space of time. Any change in soil-management which stimulates growth also, by that very fact, increases the drain of nutritive elements from the soil. Thus, researchers have noticed, for example, that the level of potassium in the soil drops rapidly when the level of nitrogen rises. This is particularly true for lawns where the natural capacity for supply of potassium is poor.

Balance of nutritive elements and diseases

It has become more and more clear that the balance of fertilizing elements helps plants to withstand the attacks of diseases. Although very few lawn diseases can be held in check merely by adjustments in the fertilizers used, disease control can be made very much easier and less costly by maintaining a strong grass growth through a well-balanced fertilizing programme.

Research has established the relationship that exists between fertilizing elements and snow-mould (Fusarium nivale), red thread (Corticium fuciforme) and stem rust (Ophiobulus graminis var. avenae). Snow-mould has spread even when the application of nitrogen has been raised as high as 20 lb (9 kg) of nitrogen per 1000 sq ft (92 m^2) per season, but the incidence of the disease has not been so marked when the extra nitrogen has been balanced with phosphorus, potassium and sulphur. On spreads of bent grass, stem rust was seven times more pronounced on spreads where there was no phosphorus, than on spreads which had had annual applications of that element.

Studies carried out at Pennsylvania State University have established that the susceptibility of bent grass and bluegrass to brown spot (Rhizactonia solani), root rot (Pythium aphanidermatum) and dollar spot (Sclerotinia homeocarpa) can be altered by various combinations of fertilizing agent and humidity. The incidence of brown spot was higher when nitrogen was increased without a similar increase in phosphorus and potassium.

At many research stations, attacks by helminthospore spots, moulds or blights (Helminthosporium spp.) were linked with an increased application of nitogen coupled with a deficiency of potash.

Researchers carried out comparative experiments with seven different nitrogen sources, each used in two different amounts on bent grass. The heavier application (10 lb (4.5 kg) of nitrogen per 1000 sq ft (92 m^2) per annum) gave better results. The strong dose of nitrogen cut down dollar spot, which led the researchers to conclude that a vigorous growth which uses up the available reserves of carbohydrates in the plant tissues lessens the plant's susceptibility to the disease. In the same study, the level of potassium in the leaves bore a close relationship to the number of disease-spots per unit of surface, and this was attributed to the influence that adequate quantities of this element had on the synthesis of proteins and the metabolism of carbohydrates.

Several factors were put forward to explain the fact that lawn-grasses were most liable to attack by diseases in unbalanced nutritional conditions, and also to explain the special relationship between nitrogen and potassium. It is clear that factors favouring a vigorous growth will improve the plant's capacity for growing, despite the presence of disease — or at least for successfully resisting the disease. Fertilizing based on nitrogen tends to produce a soft, succulent growth which may allow certain disease-producing organisms to invade the plant more easily. Conversely, potassium-based fertilizers produce a more bloated and markedly woody growth.

The interior chemical balance of the plant is another mechanism which can endow it with the capacity to resist diseases. It is known that low levels of potassium in comparison with nitrogen create an accumulation of amino-acids and amides in the plant tissues, rather than forming proteins. Some researchers deduce from this that these unassimilated substances may possibly provide an environment which is more favourable to the growth of invading disease-producing organisms.

It is certain that our present knowledge of the link between nutrition and pathogenic disorders in grasses is far from complete. Nobody has yet found an explanation of the fact that certain diseases are more severe when the fertility of the plant is raised, while others are less severe. Further research is needed on the interactions of different amounts and sources of primary, secondary and trace elements with various pathogenic organisms.

Balance of nutritive elements and climatic stress

In many areas of Canada, every kind of cultivated plant is subjected to fairly regular periods of climatic stress. Lawn-grasses are no exception to the rule. These stress situations may result from extremes of temperature, an inadequate or irregular water-supply, drought, the formation of ice, late frosts in the spring and so forth. The effects of any of these periods of stress are increased by foot-traffic.

The capacity of plants to withstand periods of stress is a function of their general vigour. More precisely, the anatomical factors — such as the size and the depth of the root system, the development of the support tissues, as well as the physiological and biochemical processes implicit in the opening of stomata, transpiration of moisture, and the building-up of reserves of carbohydrates — can determine the overall influence of the stress. Frequently, a period of stress may not be severe enough to bring about a substantial lessening of thickness of a grass, but the combination of reduced vigour, increased severity of the disease, and/or a concurrent growth of undesirable vegetable species may well aggravate the problem.

Destruction by the cold is one of the principal causes of the thinning-out of grass. It is a well-known fact that a reserve of carbohydrates is essential for survival during the winter. The reserves built up by grasses in their roots, rhizomes, stolons and the bases of their stems are there to be used during the winter; in the spring-time, when the plant comes out of the dormant state; and during the period of new growth after moving. Frequent mowing undermines the capacity of the grass to maintain sufficient reserves for periods of stress.

It is not known exactly how the balance of the nutritive elements affects the plant's resistance to cold. It is certain that the length of the root system is of some importance — which suggests the need for high levels of phosphorus and potassium.

Potassium also plays a key role in the synthesis of carbohydrates and in their movements, and also in the volume and extent of the plant's internal vessels. From this, it may be deduced that periods of winter stress exert a strain on the plant's capacity to maintain an uninterrupted flow of the essential elements.

Beard and Rieke, two researchers in Michigan, applied five different levels of nitrogen (0, 4, 8, 12, and 16 lbs of nitrogen per 1000 sq [0, 1.8, 3.5, 5.5, and 7 kg per 92 m²]) in various different combinations on a lawn of Kentucky bluegrass. At low temperatures, for all the various nitrogen levels, the maximum survival rate was obtained when the amount of potassium used was half the amount of nitrogen.

These results were obtained with soils which already contained a high enough level of available potash to make it impossible to judge what would be the effect of further applications of potash.

Dryness and high temperature are other causes of stress — particularly in the "cool-weather" species of lawn-grass. Several researchers have shown that high levels of nitrogen in the middle of summer, particularly when combined with low levels of available potassium, can increase the harmful effects of high temperatures. In certain areas — especially those where mid-summer temperatures are higher than those in most areas of Canada — applications of nitrogen should be halved during the hottest summer months, as compared with the amounts applied at other times.

Pellett and Roberts of Iowa State University have done work to determine the interaction between high temperatures and the levels of nitrogen, phosphorus and potassium applied to Kentucky bluegrass. During periods of high temperature, heavy applications of nitrogen reduced the growth of the grass to a point where it was no greater than with insignificant amounts of nitrogen. Relatively low levels of nitrogen, phosphorus and potassium did not, when applied together, have any effect on the resistance of the grass to high temperatures. However, when the level of nitrogen was high, phosphorus **reduced** resistance to the stress of temperature, while potassium **increased** it.

Other research work has shown that the balance of nutritive elements can alter a plant's ability to resist the stress associated with high temperatures and dry conditions. It has been established that plants deficient in potassium wither more easily than those which have a balanced reserve of nutritive elements. It appears that the potassium ion reduces transpiration. Studies have shown that potassium also has an influence on the closing of the stomata. Pour control of the stomata is considered to be one of the principal causes of loss of water by plants, since these microscopic openings scattered over the plant's epidermis play a major role in the development of an "air-conditioning system" for the plant during extremely hot weather.

In the present context, the vigour of grass is linked with its thickness, its general "plumpness", the strength of the individual blades and the ability of the grass to stand up to foot-traffic. It is an important factor in the preparation of the green on which the golfer makes his putts.

The blades of grass may lack firmness, hang down limply, and present a general appearance of weakness and debility. Grass lacking in vigour may not stand up straight enough, or may be insufficiently stiff, to offer a good putting surface to the golfer. Such grass will be fairly easily destroyed by foot-traffic. This type of symptom is associated with a high nitrogen content coupled with an inadequate level of potassium.

Balance of nutritive elements within plants

During the last few years experts in plant-fertilizing have begun to attach more and more importance to the amounts of essential elements ingested by plants, and to the proportions of such elements that are lost in the clippings from a mowing. These data are then used to help in the determination of what fertilizing additives are needed. Once deficiencies in the soil have been corrected, it is possible to ensure a nutritive environment suitable for any given soil or for any given species of plant, by maintaining an approximate balance between the loss of nutritive elements and the addition of compensating amounts of these same elements (such amounts, of course, being related to the effectiveness of the elements). The introduction of rapid methods of analysis, and contuning research to establish the "critical level" or "critical limit" for each of the nutritive elements, are invaluable aids in the forecasting of fertilizing needs with a higher degree of accuracy.

Analyses of many different species of grasses from many different places indicate that the approximate N-P-K relationship in the clippings is of the order of 4-1-2 or 3-1-2.

Although a determination of nutritive needs and of a suitable balance based solely on the loss of nutritive elements may really be too simplistic, several experts on grass have suggested that $N-P_2O_5-K_2O$ relationships working out around 3-1-2 or 4-1-2 are in fact the most suitable ones for a well kept lawn which is watered frequently and from which clippings are removed. Where clippings are not removed, or watering is less frequent or where the potassium content of the soil is relatively high, stronger nitrogen-potassium relationships are desirable.

Limpness of plants

From the anatomical point of view, limpness of plants is attributable to a deficiency in the development of support tissues such as cellulose. In the cases of Indian corn and rice, it has been shown that the nitrogen-potassium balance is important to stop the bending of corn stalks, and to stiffen the walls of rice stalks thus speeding up the lignification process. These results are equally applicable in the case of other vegetable species. Over and above the physical aspects, upsetting the balance of water within the plant can result in a feeble, limp and withered grass, as we have already seen.

Grass-plants produce a thick grass by the formation of stolons, rhizomes or suckers, depending on the type of grass. A balance of nutritive elements which promotes the growth of these stems is therefore very important.

In an experiment carried out in New Jersey, an application of a complete fertilizer, containing the three elements N-P-K, produced 20% more stems below the mowing-level compared with an application containing nitrogen alone. The end-result was a grass that was more vigorous, more dense and more able to stand up to foot-traffic.

Summary

The desire to produce a high-quality grass, for both its beauty and its utility, may lead a gardener to embark on a course of plant-management practices totally unsuitable for the life cycle of the grass — with the result that the plant is plunged into a struggle for survival. Although nitrogen is the key element in the production and maintenance of a high-quality grass, the rapid and impressive results that it produces may lead us to neglect other nutritive elements and their relationship with nitrogen.

A proper balance between the nutritive elements will influence many quality-factors — such as density, vigour and resistance to diseases and the stresses caused by climate and foot-traffic. Although phosphorus is of very great importance in the production of grass, particularly in the development of good root systems, nitrogen-potassium interactions appear to be the most significant factor in determining the quality of a grass. Furthermore, the greater loss of these two elements in mowing and their higher susceptibility to leaching-out as compared with that of phosphorus, indicate a relatively greater need for nitrogen and potassium in grass on which intensive care is lavished.

The balance of nutritive elements must be evaluated in the light of particular situations — such as the soil, type of grass, climate and management practices used. Any marked change in these management practices as, for example, the use of a higher proportion of controlled-release nitrogen in the sources of nutritive elements — may call for a fresh evaluation of the requirements of other elements.

MINERAL DEFICIENCIES IN THE LAWN

Although the prevention of diseases (whether pathogenic in origin, or nutritional) is a very important objective which everyone seeks to attain, it is also necessary to be able to reach a correct diagnosis when trouble strikes. Only in this way can one select the proper treatment and thus reduce the extent of possible damage. A word of warning here — when attempting the diagnosis of disorders caused by a deficiency of essential elements, it is always a wise move to have this diagnosis confirmed by a chemical analysis of the soil, the plant tissues, or both. There are plenty of analytical laboratories across Canada capable of this work. Such confirmation reduces the danger of a possible error — such as diagnosing a mineral deficiency when the real trouble is something completely different like too much water, perhaps, or too little, or extremes of temperature, lack of sun, disease or mechanical damage. However, remember that no laboratory analysis can replace vigilant attention on the site itself.

Deficiencies in primary elements

As the term "primary" suggests, these elements (nitrogen, phosphorus and potassium) are the ones which are the first to be missed in the nutrition of plants, and which must therefore be renewed in the form of fertilizers. Of the three, nitrogen is the one most frequently lacking in grass. However, with extreme pH values (whether acid or alkaline) the release of phosphorus diminishes and in these conditions a phosphorus deficiency may well develop. Furthermore, if the grass-clippings are always removed from the lawn, all three major elements tend to disappear and here the losses of nitrogen and potassium are more serious, since they exist in greater proportions in the cut grass. Here is a description of the symptoms of deficiency of the three primary elements:

Symptoms of lack of nitrogen

Beginning with the lowest, the leaves turn a greenish yellow at their bases, then go pale yellow. As the deficiency progresses, this chlorosis moves to the middle leaves and finally to those at the top; while the leaves which were first affected pass from their pale yellow colour to various shades of copper.

Symptoms of lack of phosphorus

The first sign of lack of phosphorus, as noted during the study of various types of fescue and bent grass, is the appearance of a discoloration on the tips of the lower leaves, ranging from deep green to blue-green.

Gradually, this colouring is replaced by reddish tints, which in turn go bronze, as though the grass-tips had been burned. At this point the deficiency has reached its peak. On the other hand, common bluegrass and "Merion" bluegrass never go through the blue-green phase. Instead, the first symptom is chlorosis of the leaf-tips. This resembles the chlorosis that develops in nitrogen-deficiency, with the difference that there is no initial discoloration with the leaves turning a greenish-yellow, nor does the colour of the leaves below the chlorosed area differ from that of normal leaves.

Symptoms of lack of potassium

At the beginning, lack of potassium manifests itself by the soft consistency of the leaves to the touch. First the points of the lower leaves become chlorosed, then the condition moves down along the edges, toward the base of the leaves.

Deficiencies in secondary elements

Calcium, magnesium and sulphur are called secondary nutritive elements — not because they are of secondary importance (they are just as necessary, sometimes in quantities equal to or even greater than the primary elements), but because they are generally added to the soil in a secondary fashion — i.e., they are usually used not for themselves alone, but rather as an integral part of another material which is applied to the soil for a particular reason. For example, calcium, magnesium and sulphur are found in many of the primary elements (sulphur in ammonium sulphate and calcium in the superphosphates). They are released into the soil during watering (sulphur is also deposited on the soil by rainwater). Many liming materials contain these three elements, even though contrary to popular belief, none of them is in any way necessary in the formation of a liming product. As a matter of fact, both calcium and magnesium sulphates can actually make a soil **more** acid, instead of reducing its acidity. Since these three elements are being constantly added to the soil in this "secondary" fashion, and since most soils contain them anyway as part of their basic composition, deficiencies in these secondary elements are less commonly noted than deficiencies in the major elements. Probably the deficiency most likely to be noticed is that of magnesium. This may be due to an imbalance in nutritive elements. In cases where the reserves of magnesium are low, although there is not an actual deficiency, the application of a normal quantity of calcium or potassium can reduce the amount of magnesium noticeably.

Symptoms of lack of calcium

The first sign of lack of calcium in lawn-grasses consists of a reddish-brown discoloration of the tissues lying between the veins that run along the edges of the blades of the upper leaves (which are the most yellow). Later the symptoms spread to the central vein, while the discoloration takes on light red tints. In the final phase, the points of the leaves look faded or burned.

Symptoms of lack of magnesium

The symptoms of lack of magnesium are similar to those of lack of calcium. There is one differnce, however. The first sign of a deficiency in magnesium usually appears on the lower leaves (which are the oldest) and the initial discoloration is usually a cherry red. Furthermore, in perhaps 30 to 50% of the affected leaves, the discoloration appears in blotches which run together to form bands — which do **not** appear in cases of lack of calcium.

Symptoms of lack of sulphur

The first sign of lack of sulphur in fescues and bent grasses is a paleness of the lower leaves — little different from that to be seen in nitrogen-deficiency cases except that here the colour is a somewhat paler yellowish-green. Shortly afterward, the points of the leaves take on a slightly scalded look, which spreads toward the base in a straight line along the edges of the leaves. These marginal bands gradually grow wider and wider, until finally the whole leaf is affected and withers. In the case of the bluegrasses, the central vein remains green right up to the final phase, when the entire leaf dries up. It should also be noted that "Merion" blue-grass, no matter whether it is healthy or suffering from some deficiency, is subject to mildew. If it happens to be suffering from a lack of sulphur, it then becomes extremely susceptible to the various parasites that cause mildew.

Deficiencies in trace elements

Modern methods of lawn-maintenance assign more and more importance to trace elements in the nourishment of grass than was ever the case with old-fashioned methods. As is well known, these trace elements or "minor elements", or even "micro-elements", are so called because the plant uses them in very small quantities.

In the early days of home gardening it was common practice to apply surface preparations containing either manure or organic composts. Furthermore, soils were newer, and in consequence were richer in nutritive elements. On the other hand, modern techniques have made it possible to construct lawns out of marginal-quality earth or arti-ficially-mixed soils, which usually have a particularly high sand content and low fertility, together with a minimal capacity for retention of moisture. This sort of soil, coupled with the commonly-encountered practice of over-watering, always means an increased loss of nutritive elements by leaching-out. Over-watering — especially when it is badly carried out and in areas where there is considerable foot-traffic — can also cause deficiencies in quite another fashion. The lack of aeration resulting from the compaction of the soil reduces the capacity of the plants to absorb nutritive elements, particularly nitrogen and iron. Finally, a fine rich green lawn which is beautiful all season calls for forced growth in the spring-time and in the autumn, and this in turn makes the use of trace elements in the maintenance of the grass even more important.

The symptoms of deficiency of trace elements — with the exception of chlorine — are described below. Chlorine has been deliberately omitted since it is virtually impossible to exclude that element as a soil-contaminant, and it thus seems highly improbable that a deficiency of chlorine could ever be observed. Furthermore, it should be realized that except for chlorine and molybdenum all the trace elements are immobile — i.e., they cannot normally be transported as required from the oldest tisues to the youngest. Thus, the first place trace element deficiencies are observed is in the organs of the younger plants.

This is the exact opposite of the cases of the primary and secondary elements. In these, with the single exception of calcium, all the deficiencies are first observed in the **oldest** tissues.

Symptoms of lack of iron

The first sign of lack of iron takes the form of an interveinal chlorosis (yellowing) in the youngest leaves. Unless remedial measures are taken, the whole surface of the leaf, including the central vein, becomes very pale. In a later phase the leaf turns ivory, almost white. However, there is complete absence of necrosis or decomposition of the tissues, in spite of the fact that there is an almost total lack of chlorophyll.

Symptoms of lack of manganese

In the initial phase, the symptoms of lack of manganese look very much like those of lack of iron. However, after the phase of interveinal chlorosis, plants subjected to a shortage of manganese show tiny necrosed spots on their leaves. These lesions do not attack any one part of the leaf in particular, although they are usually to be found on the lower half. If the edge is attacked, buckling takes place and the leaf becomes twisted along the side that is affected.

Symptoms of lack of zinc

The first sign of a lack of zinc is a slowing-down in the growth-rate. In the bent grasses and bluegrasses under study, the leaves affected by the deficiency became very narrow. In this condition, they looked very much like fine fescue. In addition, the affected leaves became greener and there was no doubt that this bore a relationship with the drying-out of the tissues. In common Bermuda grass, a white crystalline exudation formed at the stomata all over the whole leaf. This was probably the residue from the internal breaking-down of the tissues.

Symptoms of lack of molybdenum

Since molybdenum is mobile, the first areas to be attacked are the tips of the lower leaves. A general chlorosis spreads over this whole region, and this is followed by a faded or burned look.

Symptoms of lack of boron

The boron requirement of grass is usually lower than the requirements of all other trace elements, with the exception of molybdenum. However, unlike molybdenum, which can travel from old tissues to young tissues (which absorb it more rapidly), boron is immobile. Therefore, it must occasionally be specially supplied to the plant.

Lack of boron is characterized by a stunting of the growth areas, which leads to the formation of truncated leaves, larger nodes and shorter internodal spaces. This gives the plant the classic appearance of a rosette. Soon after the appearance of the first symptoms, streak-marks, due to interveinal chlorosis develop on the leaves.

Symptoms of lack of copper

The symptoms of lack of copper were not well defined in the grasses under study. As in the case of zinc, plants deprived of copper turn bluish, though in copper deficiency the somewhat darker discoloration is not accompanied by withering of the leaves. Also — again as in the case of zinc-deficiency — no chlorosis was noted, and from this fact these two elements must be classed separately from the other trace elements. Incidentally, it should be mentioned that in the absence of other identifying symptoms it is difficult to decide whether one is faced with a lack of boron, zinc or copper — particularly when the grass has been cut short.

Chapter II
Lawn Grasses

LAWN GRASSES

Imagine a plot covered with a lawn made of high-quality grass which is very vigorous and easily maintained. Tell yourself that this grass resists diseases, insects and drought, that it stands up well under daily use and that it only needs mowing occasionally. A dream you say? No! — this is reality, thanks to the new lawn-grasses of today which enable you to bring your lawn slowly to a state of perfection. This state of perfection may be attained in the fullness of time thanks to the continuing work of research and the selection of new varieties or "cultivars" of lawn-grasses. The work requires years of confirmatory investigation and analysis before a new grass is put onto the market and finally becomes available for use in lawns.

In the old days, grasses produced for seeding or sodding purposes also did duty as pasturage and as soil-protectors. Today, most new grasses are produced solely for lawns and meticulous care is taken over them to ensure their high quality. Unfortunately, poor-quality grasses are still available at so-called "bargain" prices. Read the label on the bag or packet of grass-seed very carefully. Generally speaking, you get what you pay for. The label should show the percentages of the different grasses in the mixture. A good grass-seed mixture should be at least 90% high-quality lawn-grasses. If the label shows a relatively high content (over 10%) of poor-quality seeds and inert matter, the mixture must be regarded as a bad buy. The same considerations apply in the case of turf. You should **not** buy poor-quality or contaminated sod.

The secret of developing a fine lawn is to choose a variety or a mixture of varieties that best suits your personal requirements, and then to maintain it properly. The quality of a finished lawn depends a great deal on the way it is laid, mowed and used. While it is always important to have a good soil, well prepared and fertilized, for your seed

The best landscaping is based on simplicity. Plants should be grouped in clumps of the same species rather than as collections of different species. The green grass supports and underlines the changing colours of the plants as the seasons pass.

or your sod, it is also essential to choose a high-quality grass that is completely suitable for your requirements.

The sort of grass you should have in your lawn depends to a large extent on where you live. For example, Kentucky bluegrass (or "meadowgrass") fescue and bent grass are very suitable for use in the fairly rigorous climatic conditions found in Canada.

Resistance to disease

Research is continually going on into the production of new varieties of grass which are resistant to diseases. Part of the problem is that diseases change, and may begin attacking varieties of grass which have always shown themselves able to resist. Again, secondary diseases may suddenly become epidemic when certain types of grass are planted in large quantity. Even "Merian" bluegrass — without any doubt the most handsome of the bluegrasses, and renowned for its resistance to disease — may be attacked by rust.

No new variety of lawn-grass is put on the market unless it shows good resistance to disease. The new species show more resistance than their predecessors — not only to the diseases themselves, but also in conditions which are highly favourable to the propagation of the diseases. This means that you can fertilize and water these new bluegrasses during the summer and maintain a vigorous growth and a rich green colour in your lawn — whereas similar treatment of the older varieties would merely encourage attacks by all sorts of diseases.

Mowing

The fact that most of the new varieties of lawn-grasses have a low, bushy growth constitutes one of their greatest

A lawn of high-quality grasses, free of weeds, forms a veritable carpet of greenery.

advantages. Thus, the new bluegrasses have shorter leaves than the old ones — which means that they can withstand a short cut very much better. Lawns made from these new grasses can be cut quite short without suffering any harm.

These new species also have other real advantages. They produce seeds which germinate more quickly, they have a greater tendency to spread by means of their rhizomes, and their colour and texture are superior.

Mixtures

When buying grass-seed, it is better to choose a mixture. In that way, one of the grasses in the mixture may turn out to be better adapted to the prevailing growth-conditions of the lawn. The mixture may consist mainly of bluegrasses, but it can also contain some fescue for shady corners, or for dry, poor soils. Rye-grass gives you a lawn quickly and is also very useful on slopes, or when you have insufficient time to lay a lawn in bluegrass.

Here are the principal mixtures of lawn-grasses recommended for various common conditions:

	Heavy and medium-heavy soils		*Light soils*	
A. Water plentiful				
	Kentucky bluegrass	70%	Kentucky bluegrass	45%
	Creeping red fescue	20%	Creeping red fescue	45%
	Perennial rye-grass	10%	'Redtop' bent grass	10%
B. Water scare				
	Kentucky bluegrass	60%	Creeping red fescue	60%
	Creeping red fescue	30%	Kentucky bluegrass	25%
	Perennial rye-grass	10%	Canada bluegrass	15%

Numerous species

There are many species of lawn-grass, although not all of them are suitable for use in Canada. Most lawn-grasses grow better in a cool, moist climate than in areas where the climate is predominantly hot and dry.

Lawns generally consist of a mixture of several lawn-grasses. The actual proportions depend chiefly on the location of the lawn — i.e., whether it is sited mainly in the sun or mainly in the shade.

Most lawn mixtures sold for private properties are made up by seedsmen. To ensure satisfaction, deal only with a gardening centre or a seedmerchant whom you can trust. In addition, be forewarned that generally speaking the ordinary mixtures sold by stores that do not specialize in horticulture are often almost worthless because they contain grass-seeds which have no possibility of surviving in certain types of soil and certain climatic conditions. This type of

This dense, thick lawn is like a putting green. It consists of a mixture of high-quality permanent lawn-grasses such as Kentucky bluegrass, creeping red fescue, bent grass and rye-grass.

seed is also responsible to a large extent for the high price
of grass-seed mixtures in general.

False economy

If you have acquired a good knowledge of the various
lawn-grasses and their growth-characteristics, you can spare
yourself a lot of useless work and avoid wasting time and
money. Never buy a cheap mixture in order to save money.
Such a purchase is very poor business, for in the long run
it will require much hard work to make a decent lawn out
of it. Also, remember that it costs more to improve a poor
lawn than it does to keep a fine lawn looking its best.

The bluegrasses

The best-known of the bluegrasses are Kentucky bluegrass or "meadowgrass" (Poa pratensis), Canada bluegrass (Poa compressa) and annual bluegrass (Poa annua).
These have many species, sub-species and varieties. They
are considered to be the best lawn-grasses by virtue of
their perfect green colour, their fine texture and a root-
system which propagates itself in the soil to produce a
compact turf. When they first start growing in the spring,
these grasses grow close to the soil. Then, as the season
progresses, their growth takes on increased vigor.

However, during the really hot weather of July and
August these grasses go into a dormant or semi-dormant
state. Unless the summer is exceptionally cool and damp,
or the lawn is watered freely, bluegrasses dry out, stiffen and
turn brownish. They will remain so until the onset of the
cool autumn evenings. Then the grass begins to grow again
— slowly if it is a dry autumn, more quickly if it is wet.
The grass will stay green until the first frost.

Kentucky bluegrass

There are certain inconvenient points about Kentucky bluegrass which must also be mentioned. To begin with, the seed of this grass germinates slowly and it takes a long time to get a lawn properly "started". That particular fault is usually corrected by mixing in a quick-growing lawn-grass such as common bent grass (Agrostis alba), which gives a nice green growth that lasts until the bluegrass comes up. Next, Kentucky bluegrass does not grow well in the shade, in a soil lacking in nutritive elements, in a dry soil or in a badly-drained one. Furthermore, this grass does not produce a turf thick enough to stifle dandelions or other lawn weeds. Much patience is required to make a lawn out of bluegrass. It takes several years before the grass is thick enough and strong enough to get rid of weeds.

There are, however, some positive aspects. Kentucky bluegrass grows well in a good garden loam, in full sunlight and at moderate temperatures.

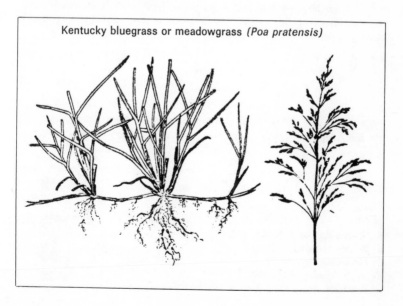

Kentucky bluegrass or meadowgrass *(Poa pratensis)*

The Kentucky bluegrass cultivar is probably the best known and the most widely used of the lawn-grasses. This is a long-lived perennial, endowed with a lovely green colour and a pleasant texture. By virtue of its vigorous rhizomes, it produces a thick, dense turf. All bluegrasses prefer a loamy or clayey soil which is well fertilized. In dry weather, Kentucky bluegrass turns brown and seems about to die, but all that is happening is that the grass is "taking a rest". However, this produces an unwelcome side-effect, as it encourages the invasion of weeds. On the other hand, Kentucky bluegrass offers more resistance to disease than other species — particularly to helmintho-spore spots, moulds or blights (Helminthosporium spp.).

Diagram to illustrate the growth of Kentucky bluegrass

The diagram illustrates a complete season's growth of Kentucky blue-grass. First come little blades in mid-April which are growing vigorous-ly by the end of April. May and June are the flowering months. During the extreme heat of July and August the grass is in a dormant state. The cool days of September and October restore its vigour, and the grass regains its rich green colour.

| MID-APRIL | END-APRIL | MAY | JUNE | JULY | AUGUST | SEPT. | OCT. |

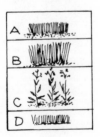

KEY:
A. Blades just beginning to grow.
B. Blades growing vigorously.
C. Flowering: the height of the stem is an indication of the vigour of growth.
D. Dormant state: the turf is dry and hard.

However, it is very vulnerable to powdery mildew, especially in shady places. Although it is fairly susceptible to rust, this bluegrass resists well when it is grown on well-fertilized and well-irrigated soil.

There are several varieties, a few of which are described below:

Kenblue: This lawn-grass produces a luxuriant growth in the spring-time and in the autumn, but comparatively little in mid-summer. It is susceptible to leaf spot, which slows down its growth considerably and turns it brown at the beginning of the summer. Although it is resistant to leaf rust, it falls an easy victim to powdery mildew, which can cause considerable damage in shaded locations. 'Kenblue' grass stands up well enough under daily use, and is

Three vigorous plants of improved varieties of Kentucky bluegrass. These specimens of lawn-grass, with their well-developed roots, will stand up to repeated mowing of the lawn throughout the summer.

The new varieties of Kentucky bluegrass produce much denser tufts — and hence a thicker lawn.

found in most of the grass mixtures used in Michigan, where the soils are in general poorly fertilized. This variety was formerly known under the name of 'Common' bluegrass. However, 'Common' is a category of seed, and not a specific variety.

Delta: This variety of Kentucky bluegrass is similar to 'Kenblue' and like 'Kenblue', it is susceptible to helmintho-spore diseases, although it recovers from their attacks much more quickly. It is fairly resistant to stem rust and powdery mildew. The 'Delta' variety has exceptionally vigorous creeping roots, and also recovers fairly quickly from the effects of dryness. Its growth is reasonably erect.

Merion: When it is properly cultivated, this next variety of bluegrass produces a very thick grass of a high quality and medium density, with broad, deep green leaves. Its chief value lies in its resistance to leaf spot, which enables it to produce a better growth during the summer than other varieties such as 'Kenblue', 'Delta', 'Park' and 'Newport'. This bluegrass is very vulnerable to powdery mildew, which can cause extensive defoliation in shaded locotions. Stem rusts are also a problem with 'Merion', but this can be overcome by the use of a fertilizer containing sufficient nitrogen.

Baron: This is a bluegrass with deep green leaves. It gives a good thick grass, and is well suited to our Canadian climate. It takes root easily, produces numerous rhizomes, becomes green and grows rapidly in the spring. 'Baron' resists weeds and leaf spot very satisfactorily. It is one of the most popular bluegrasses.

'Merion' bluegrass, on the left, grows much thicker than ordinary Kentucky bluegrass.

The 'Baron' variety exemplifies the value of the new species of Kentucky bluegrass selected for their relatively short growth, their resistance to diseases, and their abundance of roots and rhizomes.

Fylking: This bluegrass was recently created in Sweden and according to all reports is proving itself extremely useful. It has undergone an extensive series of tests both in Canada and in the United States. It establishes itself more quickly than 'Merion' does, and by virtue of its very vigorous rhizome system it recovers very quickly from diseases. It produces a very thick turf which is highly resistant to the attacks of weeds, leaf spot, streaky rust and stem and dactyl rust. 'Fylking' leaves are narrower than those of 'Merion' and it is therefore finer. Since the sheath of the leaves is shorter than the tuft at the base of the lower leaves, it can grow even if cut as low as ½ inch (1.5 cm). It seems to resist dryness a little better than 'Merion', although its fertilizing needs are the same. Among its disadvantages are a rapid accumulation of culm if the grass is not well cared

Six varieties of Kentucky bluegrass compared for growth. From left to right: 'Baron', 'Arboretum', 'Sodco', 'Pennstar', 'Fylking', 'Nugget'.

for, and a shaggy appearance if the grass has been cut irregularly or allowed to grow more than 2 inches (5 cm) high.

Windsor: This bluegrass has deep green leaves and grows rather slowly. It is fairly susceptible to leaf spot, powdery mildew and rust. Just like 'Merion', 'Windsor' responds well to strong applications of nitrogen.

Mixing two or three varieties of Kentucky bluegrass for the creation of a lawn is a practice which is becoming more and more common. It has the advantage of offering a wider range of resistance to diseases and a readier adaptation to the surroundings. Mixing two or more varieties can be termed a desirable technique when the grass-seed is likely to be subjected to widely differing methods of cultivation, depending on where it is sold. In this case, that part of the mixture which adapts best to a particular local condition will become the predominant species in that locality.

The exceptional quality of the 'Baron' variety of Kentucky bluegrass has been demonstrated in numerous tests carried out in different lawn-grass research centres in both America and Europe. It takes root well, and produces numerous rhizomes which form a dense, thick lawn that stands up well under wear.

Canada bluegrass

Canada bluegrass is the only variety of bluegrass which is actually blue. It is perennial, and its underground stems, which spread vigorously, put out numerous branches in all directions. It will grow on many soils where other bluegrasses will not grow — hard, poor, clayey, sandy-clayey and so on.

Annual bluegrass

Annual bluegrass produces a shorter grass than Kentucky bluegrass. It is often classed as a weed, because it will

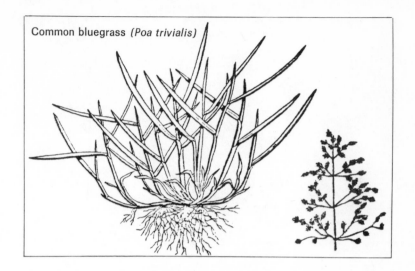
Common bluegrass *(Poa trivialis)*

grow in soil felt to be too damp and too hard-packed to permit the growth of other lawn-grasses. Wherever this bluegrass appears should be well fertilized and sown with good-quality lawn-grass to replace the dead plants of the annual bluegrass. Annual bluegrass does better in shaded locations, along foot-paths and close to buildings. It is a very low-growing plant, rarely exceeding a height of 3 or 4 inches (7.5 to 10 cm). This grass attains its full growth in May, then it turns yellow, dries up and disappears completely in the summer, leaving seeds which will grow the following spring.

Common bent grass

Common or stoloniferous bent grass (Agrostis alba) is used principally as a "plant-protector" in bluegrass lawns. It produces a rapid growth of greenery which gives a handsome look to the lawn while the bluegrass is getting established. However, this bent grass — which is perennial —

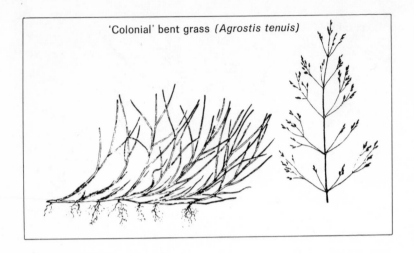

'Colonial' bent grass *(Agrostis tenuis)*

becomes progressively shaggier and more vigorous year by year, until it spoils the look of the lawn. It is a plant with a creeping growth, which does reasonably well in shaded spots and on acid soils, and it may be cut very short.

Creeping bent grass

The 'Penncross' variety of creeping bent grass (Agrostis paludris) was created at the Agricultural Experimental Station of Pennsylvania by the late Professor H. Burton Musser. It came from a chance crossing of the first-generation offspring of three parent grasses propagated by vegetable means.

'Penncross' gives a dense, finely-textured grass, and with normal care it has less tendency to produce long stems and turn into culm — as is the case with the 'Seaside' variety and other creeping bent grasses obtained by sowing seeds. 'Penncross' should be kept fairly dry because it has a tendency to take on a downy look, and is also easily damaged if it is too strongly stimulated by fertilizing or by over-vigorous irrigation. Although it is not very resistant to

'Highland' bent grass gives a dense, velvety lawn. However, this lawn-grass calls for careful attention, a damp location and frequent mowing.

diseases, it has a fairly high tolerance for the normal grass diseases. Because of its characteristic rapid growth, it overcomes their attacks and recovers quickly.

The 'Seaside' variety is admittedly more popular than 'Penncross' — mainly because it is the only grass of the Agrostid family available as a source of seed. The economic advantages of sowing seed, as opposed to planting stolons, are obvious. 'Seaside' produces a grass of lower quality than 'Penncross' — lower, too, than several creeping stolon-iferous varieties such as 'Toronto c-15'. It has a tendency to degenerate into culm rather rapidly and to produce a surface which is both downy and irregular. It is somewhat suscep-tible to disease — in particular to snow-mould. Because of its relatively slow rate of growth, it recovers slowly from an attack of disease.

Rye-grass

The two main species of rye-grass are English rye-grass

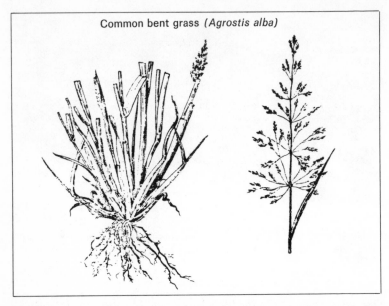

Common bent grass *(Agrostis alba)*

(Lollium perenne) and Italian rye-grass (Lollium multi-florum). They are absolutely identical except for the fact that the former (Lollium perenne) is a perennial, while the latter (Lollium multiflorum) is an annual. Both of them look like Kentucky bluegrass, since they grow in little tufts.

English rye-grass grows in sprawling tufts which consist of secondary tufts bound together by the outspread branches of the root-stocks. Italian rye-grass is similar to the English variety. Its tufts look much the same, but the stems are higher and more delicate. Like common bent grass, these plants are useful primarily as "plant-protectors" since their major quality is their powerful growth.

By themselves, these grasses will not produce a handsome lawn. They last only until they are stifled by more persistent grasses. Furthermore, they are not grasses that are easy to mow. Even though they look attractive at the beginning of the season, when the really hot days of summer come along their leaves begin to bend back, and then they

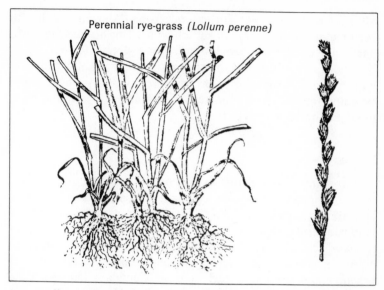
Perennial rye-grass *(Lollum perenne)*

turn yellow. Fortunately, this condition corrects itself at the end of September and they turn a beautiful deep green once again.

Generally speaking, English rye-grass (Lollium perenne), which is tufted and short-lived, is used mainly as a cover-grass in Canada, because of its rapid germination and growth. This enables it to protect higher-quality species which germinate and grow less rapidly.

The 'Norlea' variety was created by the Canadian Federal Ministry of Agriculture. It is hardier in the winter-time than other perennial rye-grasses and does not wither so quickly after a close cut. It is outstanding on two counts: first, its extraordinarily rapid growth; and second, its brilliant green colour which lasts late into the autumn. Since its texture and its colour look very much like those of 'Merion' bluegrass, these two grasses are often used together. However, 'Norlea' grows more rapidly than 'Merion'; and if the lawn is fertilized and watered heavily, and the grass is cut irregularly in mid-summer — as tends to happen with the lawns of private homes — 'Norlea' outstrips 'Merion', with the result that the grass looks rather ugly. 'Norlea' can be quite useful for controlling erosion on slopes alongside foot-paths, but there are other grasses that do the job equally well and will in addition resist dryness and grow well in a soil which contains few nutritive elements — which is usually the case in such locations.

Fescue

Creeping red fescue (Festuca rubra) is an excellent lawn-grass. It produces a fine compact carpet, resists dryness and stands up well to shade and constant usage. It has a very slow rate of growth and therefore takes a long time to recover from injuries. The 'Olds' and 'Duraturf' varieties or cultivars are of Canadian origin and supply almost all the fescue seed produced and sold in Canada. 'Pennlawn', a cultivar produced at the Agricultural Experimental Station of Pennsylvania by the late Professor Musser, is acknowledged as being superior to other fescues for its creeping capacity (it spreads through the soil by means of its underground rhizomes) and for its resistance to weeds and diseases. Its leaves are narrower than those of other creeping fescues and they give a fine, compact grass that can be cut to a height of 1 inch (2.5 cm).

The use of red fescue, or of a mixture of red fescue and Kentucky bluegrass, is indicated for: (a) cooler climates (b) shaded locations (c) soils containing a high proportion of sand.

The 'Pennlawn' variety is the one to choose when resistance to dryness and the effects of low temperature are required.

It is the best grass for laying underneath trees — i.e., in places where the soil is dry and where the sun never penetrates. This lawn-grass does equally well in sandy soils where most grasses cannot survive. Since it is different

Creeping red fescue *(Festuca rubra)*

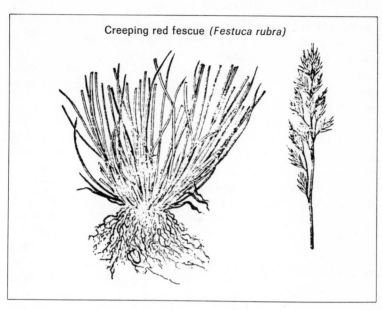

Tall fescue *(Festuca arundinacea)*

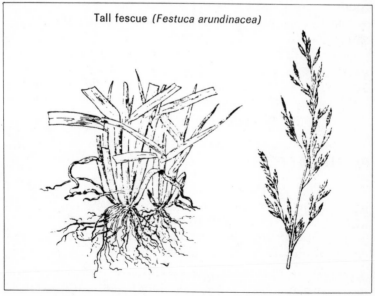

from other fescues, both as to colour and as to method of growth, it cannot be grown with these other grasses. Red fescue grows in tufts and during the dry spells of summer it becomes very stiff and is difficult to cut. Warm, humid temperatures do not suit it, nor can it survive in the intense heat of mid-summer.

The tall fescue 'Kentucky 31' (Festuca elatrior arundinaceae) is a coarse variety, resistant to dryness, which grows on certain soils. It is the commonly-used grass in Kentucky for forage and pasturage purposes. Since it grows well on poor, dry soils, it is very suitable for airfields, road borders, sports fields, factory surrounds and the "rough" on golf courses — in fact, anywhere where mowing and maintenance will be reduced to a minimum on grounds of economy, or for any other reason. It has been used successfully with vetch of the 'Coronilla' species (Coronilla varia) along the sloping sides of cut-and-fill roadwork, where soil-stabilizing mixtures are needed. In other locations, it has even been used with 'Merion' bluegrass for exercise grounds. 'Kentucky 31' tall fescue is a slightly finer grass than 'Alta' tall fescue. To obtain the best results, 'Kentucky 31' and 'Alta' should be sown quite thickly — say 7 to 10 lb (3 to 4.5 kg) per 1,000 sq ft (92 m^2). Both of these will give a good coarse surface that will stand up well under use. They should be grown on well-drained and moderately-fertilized soils, and should be cut to a height of 2½ to 3 inches (6 to 7.5 cm).

PLANT CARPETS

Are you tired of mowing your lawn? Have you been trying to get lawn-grass to grow in places where it simply will not take? The solution to these lawn problems is to use plants with broad evergreen leaves and other plants with deciduous leaves to form "plant carpets".

There are several of these plants available now and all indications are that in the near future there will be many more of them. When they are used in the right way in suitable locations, these plants require far less attention than grass does. Certain species will form a lovely uniform carpet over the soil, and will last for many years without requiring much care at all.

Admittedly, of all the hardy perennial plant carpets, permanent lawn-grasses are the most resistant and can be counted on with the most confidence. Grass is still unbeatable if it is properly cultivated and fertilized and properly protected against invasion by weeds and the depredations of insect pests. However, there are many places where grass will not grow properly and where its carpeting never manages to look attractive — e.g., under trees which throw wide, heavy shadows.

Creeping myrtle *(Vinca minor)* is an excellent carpeting plant for shaded locations.

Furthermore, there are many damp sites and dry places where grass cannot survive. Again, there are sharp or rocky slopes on which the grass manages to take hold, but finds it hard to thrive. Then there are "impossible" places, such as beneath the overhanging eaves of a roof. Here, the grass **can** grow if it is watered often enough — but most of the time it just dies from neglect. Therefore, plants used as vegetable carpets must be capable of withstanding the sun or the shade as well as inadequate watering.

What is a plant carpet?

Quite simply, a plant carpet consists of plants that cover the ground completely. In this connection, one's thoughts go automatically to grass. While grass is certainly one of the best carpeting plants, it does have limitations in its use, depending on the purpose for which it has been planted and on local conditions.

Ideal carpeting plants should possess the following characteristics:

(1) Short growth, not exceeding 12 inches (30 cm)

(2) Good growth performance and good appearance, with a minimum of maintenance

(3) Cover sufficiently thick, and able to ward off attacks by weeds

(4) Interesting appearance maintained throughout all four seasons of the year, not merely one or two

(5) Ability to grow in locations where other plants would die

The carpeting plants mentioned below conform very closely to the requirements listed above. I have deliberately chosen the most difficult circumstances and locations (which are, after all, what you will usually encounter) and the plants best suited for these conditions.

Let me stress here that these plants grow well, not because of the disadvantageous situations in which we place them but because they tolerate these situations better than other plants could. The soil should be well drained and adequately fertilized. During its preparation, a sufficient quantity of organic matter should be worked into it in order to give it a good basic structure. Then a 5-20-20 fertilizer should be mixed in with the top 6 inches (15 cm) of the soil, in quantities dictated by the needs of the soil. During the actual planting, and thereafter until they are well established, the plants should receive the most careful attention. Just as with any other plant, final success depends on the degree of care exercised while the plant is "settling in".

A minimum of care

Plant carpets require almost no maintenance at all — provided, of course, that you have chosen the right plant for the particular conditions. Once they have taken hold properly, these plants will cover the soil fairly quickly. After that, maintenance boils down to an occasional hoeing and trimming the edges of the area covered by the carpet.

However, in one or two cases you may have to nip off the flowers as they wither and die, or remove fruit-bearing stems. Other plants may require trimming every now and then to keep them looking as beautiful as possible.

A word of warning

Some of the plants mentioned here may prove difficult to find. True, all — or nearly all — of the catalogues put out by seedsmen and gardening centres will list creeping myrtle (Vinca minor), Japanese spurge (Pachysandra terminalis) and wintercreeper (Euonymus fortunei), but you may have to do some serious looking before you succeed in finding some of the other plants. However, you may be lucky enough to find that some of them are growing wild in your own particular region. You may even find some of them being sold as rock-garden plants.

Aegopodium or bishop's-weed is an ideal covering for both sunny and shady spots.

Let me warn you against certain plants which behave more like weeds than anything else. An example is aegopodium or bishop's-weed (Aegopodium podagraria 'Variegata'). This plant makes an excellent plant carpet and is very frequently used for that purpose. However, only too often it will spread to other areas of the garden where it can cause a lot of trouble to other plants. It can prove very difficult to get rid of, and since it spreads by means of its seeds it may invade flowerbeds, rockeries and all sorts of other places — and may well end up dominating the entire garden.

Very sunny localities

Although the list of carpeting plants suitable for very sunny places is the longest of them all, you may not always find them listed in seedsmen's and gardening centres' catalogues, since they are not sold as carpeting plants. They are more likely to be considered rock-garden plants.

Indigenous bearberry (Arctostaphylos uva-ursi) is the best plant to produce a covering on soil exposed to full sunlight, especially if it is sandy. This plant is not only a carpeting plant with evergreen leaves and a very handsome appearance, which grows only a few inches high, it has the additional advantage that it produces lovely shining fruit in the autumn.

At the present time, bearberry may not be found in adequate quantities at your local seedsmen's. However, this situation is bound to correct itself in the near future and you will be able to buy as much as you need. It can be propagated by slips of green wood during the early days of summer, or — provided reasonable care is taken — it can be transplanted directly from wild plants in clumps or strips, early in the spring-time before its first growth.

In dry, sandy places exposed to the sun, fernleaf yarrow (Achillea tomentosa) grows very well. From the end of May until early September, flat bunches of bright yellow flowers make their appearance above a foliage which looks like ferns.

Japanese spurge *(Pachysandra terminalis)* — its evergreen leaves form a carpeting of green. This plant is excellent for covering slopes where there is plenty of shade. It may also be used in sunny and semi-shaded locations.

The effect is quite striking. After the flowering season, the dead flowers should be removed so that the carpet of leaves can be seen in all its beauty. This plant may be used to advantage along pathways, or between stepping-stones. A moderate amount of foot-traffic seems to cause no serious damage. It should not be used on really large areas, since its stolons do not let it cover the ground quickly enough.

Wormwood (Artemisia var. 'Silver Mound') is particularly suitable for sandy soils where it produces broad carpets of silvery tufts.

Ground ivy (Nepeta hederacea) grows like a weed wherever you put it. However, it produces a very lovely carpet and needs only to be clipped every now and then to stop it from spreading too far.

Yellow stonecrop (Sedum acre) is a delicate carpeting plant for slopes which are very dry and badly exposed to the sun.

Snow-in-summer (Cerastium tomentosum), moss pink (Phlox subulata) and various pinks (Dianthus species) are flowering rock-garden plants which are also very useful as plant carpets in sunny locations, on slopes and anywhere else where grass is difficult to cut.

Creeping cotoneaster (Cotoneaster adpressa) is a beautiful delicate shrub with sprigs that spread out close to the ground carrying leaves that look like necklaces.

Shady locations

One of the best plants for shaded spots — e.g., underneath Norwegian maples — or for where an asphalt road or the like surrounds a garden, is bishop's weed (Aegopodium podagraria 'Variegata'). This is a highly resistant plant which reaches a height of 8 to 14 inches (20 to 35 cm). It produces flattish flowers in May and June, which look rather like those of carrots. They are not very attractive and it is better to cut them away.

This plant spreads rapidly by means of rhizomes and, as pointed out earlier, if it is not properly controlled it can become a weed. It retains its good looks even if it is cut with a lawn mower once during the summer. It grows both in the sun and in the shade, and in poor soils as well as in good. During the winter the plant is killed down to ground level and the carpet of leaves disappears until the following spring.

For general use, it is hard to find a better plant than creeping myrtle (Vinca minor). This is a carpeting plant of many uses. It grows in tufts with evergreen leaves, it rarely exceeds 8 inches (20 cm) in height and it can take full sunlight or partial shade. Its lilac-blue flowers are among the first to appear in the garden, at the end of April. Its lustrous deep-green leaves keep their attractiveness all year round. If you feel it is too common a plant for you, why not try one of its many varieties?

There is Vinca minor alba, which has white flowers, while those of Vinca minor purpurea are purple. Then there are the multiplex varieties with double flowers, and the Aureovariegata which have leaves streaked with yellow.

Ordinary creeping myrtle is so widely used simply because it is one of the best carpeting plants available. It is hardly subject to disease at all, or to any other plant scourges; and it grows with a minimum of attention. It is usually in reasonably plentiful supply at local nurseries.

Japanese spurge (Pachysandra terminalis), which produces an attractive foliage, is perhaps the best carpeting plant to grow underneath trees.

For large and very shaded areas where grass lasts only a short time, English ivy (Hedera helix) is the perfect answer, and will grow very well. This creeping plant with evergreen leaves reaches a height of 6 to 8 inches (15 to 20 cm). Once it is properly established, it will very quickly cover a large area with a thick carpet of greenery. When it is not being used as a soil-covering, it does not stand up very well to climatic conditions other than in sheltered areas

Japanese spurge *(Pachysandra terminalis)* is particularly suitable for surfaces that are mainly in the shade — though it also stands up well to the sun.

such as the Niagara Peninsula. It prefers a rich, moist loam and it should not be exposed continually to full sunlight during the winter. Among the varieties of English ivy, mention should be made of large-leaved ivy (Hedera helix baltica) and small-leaved ivy (Hedera helix 'Thorndale').

Drug speedwell (Veronica officinalis), originally from Ontario, is very useful in natural plantations of spruce, pine and white cedar. This plant with evergreen leaves rarely grows higher than 4 inches (10 cm) except during its flowering-period, and it remains a brilliant lustrous green all through the growth season, without needing any maintenance. It is a creeping plant, putting down roots at each node and forming a covering thick enough to discourage weeds very successfully. It stands up reasonably well under foot-traffic. Research has shown that in a watery solution it grows well at pH values between 4.0 and 7.5. It has been tested on experimental lots over a period of three years, in full sunlight and in shade, and has acted very satisfactorily. If you are unable to find it in your local nurseries, you can use it in the wild state — either in the form of tufty plants, or by taking slips of green wood during the growing season.

For damp and acid soils

Damp and acid soils are most frequently encountered in badly-drained areas. As the first step — before anything else — it is essential that you try to improve the drainage, thereby giving yourself a considerably wider range of plants to choose from. Bog rosemary (Andromeda polifolium) and the various types of plantain-lily (Hosta species) are very suitable for damp and acid soils. Another plant that grows well in most acid soils is reynoutia fleeceflower (Polygonum reynoutia). This grows up to 2 ft (61 cm) in height and is a reasonably attractive plant, with gaudy red fruit.

Close to water

As a general rule it is difficult to get grass to grow along the banks of streams, around pools, or in marshy soils lying in full sunlight or partial shade. These are the sort of places where you should put moneywort or creeping Jenny (Lysimachia nummularia). Brilliant yellow flowers cover a foliage some 2 inches (5 cm) high, from May to September. Creeping Jenny takes hold quickly and covers the ground with stolons which put down roots at each node. It spreads equally well in moist or well-drained soils and produces a thick foliage through which few weeds can make their way. Along rocks and at the edges of ponds its long fronds hang down gracefully, trailing down into the water. This plant is easy to establish and easy to maintain.

Temporary cover

It is often desirable to put down temporary cover in a new arrangement of shrubs, or perhaps to give some colour during the spring and summer to an area where normally nothing can be grown except the shortest of green plants. Knotweed (Polygonum sagittatum) is a low creeping plant which is grown from seed in the spring and is killed by cold weather in the autumn. It develops very quickly, rarely exceeding a height of 3 inches (7.5 cm). Small rose-coral flowers and bronzed green leaves afford an excellent background for flowering plants. It is often used together with lavender-cotton (Santolina chamaecyparissus) as the base for mixed arrangements at summer flower-shows.

Less well-known species

You should also consider getting some other, less well-known, species. Worth mentioning in this group is the double-flowered creeping buttercup (Ranunculus repens 'Pleniflorus'), which produces quick-growing stolons — up to 2 ft (61 cm) or more in one year. Canby pachistima (Paxistima canbyi) is a shrub with semi-evergreen leaves, which reaches a height of 18 inches (45 cm.)

Chamaedrys germander (Teucrium chamaedrys) is a very simple plant with dense foliage which attains a height of 10 inches (25 cm). Creeping Jenny (Lysimachia nummularia) is another carpeting plant which grows well in the shade. Nor must we overlook the varieties of Euonymus such as wintercreeper (Euonymus fortunei) or alpine epimedium (Epimedium alpinum), a pretty little plant with a very thick foliage and red and yellow flowers which look like miniature columbinea.

Chapter III

Preparation and Renovation

Chapter 11

PRESERVATION
and RESTORATION

Preparing a lawn

A beautiful deep-green lawn is the dream of every amateur gardener! This is an ideal which, for far too many people, seems quite unattainable. Yet it is relatively simple to create beautiful grass. The most important thing is not to neglect any of the factors which are essential for success.

No one can deny that the beauty of any garden depends mainly on the lawn. The lawn is the foreground of the house — the feature of any residence worthy of the name. Beautiful green grass, with the appropriate plants to set it off, improves the appearance of a property beyond belief and does a great deal to help raise its market value.

The lawn is the 'better half' of a successful landscaping layout. Without a high-quality lawn, trees, shrubs and flowerbeds lose much of their aesthetic value. Multi-coloured flowers are shown up in all their beauty when they are displayed against a fine, healthy green lawn.

When it comes to laying a lawn, it is essential to pay particular attention to the underground drainage, the slope and grading of the ground, the type of soil and its preparation and fertilization. In addition, only high-quality sod or guaranteed seed must be used.

If a single one of these factors is forgotten, or if the fundamental principles are neglected, the results obtained will inevitably be disappointing. Those who have failed in their attempts to create a lawn may attribute their lack of success to one of the following causes: a poor soil, sowing carried out at the wrong time, the use of poor-quality seed or turf infested with weeds, a location with too much shade or faulty care (e.g., cutting the grass too short, not fertilizing it enough, inadequate watering or failure to deal with weeds).

Preparing the ground

To create a fine, handsome lawn the first essential is to prepare a proper seed-bed. Remove all rocks and rubbish in the soil and on the surface of the ground. Also, if the soil has vegetable matter near the surface, this should be removed to beyond the edges of the future lawn. Then grade the ground so that it drains away from the house.

One method of dealing with the problem of unsatisfactory soil is simply to dig out the whole area to a depth of 6 to 18 inches (15 to 45 cm), remove the soil and take it somewhere else, then replace it with good surface soil.

However, in my opinion, unless the soil is so cluttered up with rubbish that it is quite impossible to clean it up or improve it, it would be better to retain it and make a real effort to turn it into a soil as near the ideal as possible. Besides, only too often the replacement garden soil brought from outside will turn out to be hardly any better than your own original soil. While we are on the subject, let me stress the importance of extreme caution when you buy soil. Deal

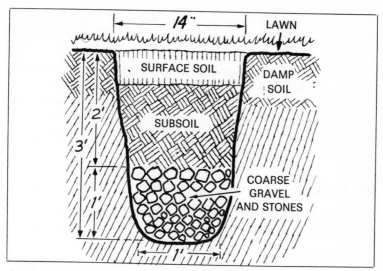

A trench helps to remove the surplus water which accumulates in the low areas of a property — e.g., at the foot of terrace.

Short lengths of ½-inch (1.7 m) pipe, inserted every 2 feet (60 cm) in the mortar above the first course of a supporting-wall, allow effective drainage at the foot of a slope.

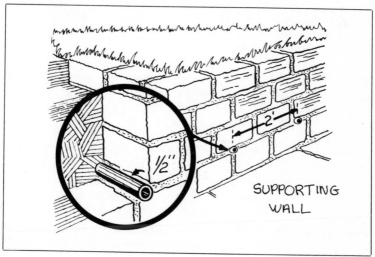

only with firms or individuals of established reputation, preferably members of the Seedmen's and Landscape Gardeners' Association.

Whether you are sowing seed or laying sod, the first step to take in the creation of a lawn is to give the ground a proper slope. It is not enough that the general contouring of the property as a whole should be pleasing to the eye. It must be graded in such a fashion that the water runs away from the house and its surroundings.

Drainage

Once the ground has been cleaned up, the next step is to give it proper drainage. Grading to a suitable slope will take

Sketch of an underground drainage-system in a typical lot. Note that the many side-drains, 3 or 4 inches (7.5 to 10 cm) in diameter, branching off to different areas of the lot, are connected to a central collector, 5 or 6 inches (12.5 to 15 cm) in diameter. When the soil of a lot is sufficiently damp to need a system such as this, the ends of the side-branches must lie no more than 20 feet (6 m) from the central collector. You must also ensure that this collector discharges into the municipal drainage system, or into some other spot from which excess water can be easily removed.

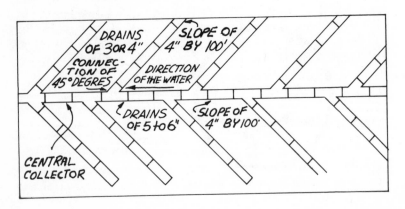

care of surface drainage. However, should the subsoil be impermeable (loam, clay or hard-packed earth), it would be wise to improve the drainage by installing 4-inch (10 cm) drain-pipes. Lay the pipes in rows spaced 15 to 20 ft (4.5 to 6 m) apart, at a depth of 2½ to 3 ft (75 to 90 cm), with a slope of 2 to 4 inches in 50 ft (5 to 10 cm in 15 m).

Good drainage provides a physical condition in the soil which is favourable to the development of the roots of grass-plants. Furthermore, it is known that layers of underground water cause serious damage to lawn-grasses.

When grading the ground avoid forming terraces if at all possible. Remember to fill in all holes and depressions in the surface. That done, the next step is to loosen up the subsoil to a depth of 5 or 6 inches (12.5 to 15 cm). Then grade the surface and add at least 4 inches (10 cm) of good arable earth, which you should fertilize by mixing in a complete chemical fertilizer in the proportions of 30 pounds (13 kg) of 6-9-6, 20 pounds (9 kg) of 12-4-8, or 15 pounds (6.8 kg) of 24-12-6 per 1000 sq ft (92 cm²).

The surface soil

The subsoil should be covered with a layer of 4 to 6 inches (10 to 15 cm) of vegetable earth. If the surface soil was trucked away following construction of the house, or if there is not enough vegetable earth, then it is essential to obtain a sufficient quantity of good garden soil. Even if the cost seems high, do not hesitate, for without an arable soil a really beautiful lawn will be a matter of luck.

Organic matter

If the surface soil is insufficiently rich in humus you should add some organic matter — manure, compost, peat-moss or rotted leaves — mixing it well into the soil at the

same time as you add the chemical fertilizer. You will probably be unable to obtain any well-rotted farm manure, which is fairly rare, and it may also be difficult to find any compost or rotted leaves. In this case — like the majority of amateur gardeners — simply use peat-moss. The correct quantity is 2 sacks per 1000 sq ft (92 m²) of surface. I should perhaps mention that it is an excellent substitute, providing all the organic matter needed and also releasing a certain amount of nitrogen as it decomposes.

After loosening up the soil, rake the surface layer to get rid of bumps and dips. Continue raking until the soil is broken down into particles not exceeding ¼ to ½ inch (0.6 to 1.5 cm) in diameter. This will give the best possible surface for sowing grass-seed.

Sowing

Sod or seed

In order to lay a lawn as quickly as possible, it is easier to lay sod rather than to sow grass-seed. However, the best time for sowing is in August and September.

Sowing is in fact the less expensive method. It gives much more uniform results and furthermore avoids the problem of weeds. Let me stress here that a fine, permanent grass takes more time to establish itself than a coarser, temporary grass. But once established and properly maintained it is a constant source of satisfaction.

Mid-August is the ideal time to lay a lawn by sowing seed. Once again, this method, though less rapid than sodding, is more economical and from many points of view more satsifactory.

Good-quality seed

If you are sowing a lawn, it is absolutely essential to use a high-quality seed of guaranteed composition. Do **not** buy haphazardly; do **not** take the advice of anyone who suggests that you use millet seed or some cheap mixture. If you want to succeed at your first attempt, and not have to start all over

Preparing the soil Whatever grass-seed you are using, you will get the best results in a soil of uniform texture. The soil should be moist, but not damp, when you dig it up or turn it over. To ensure a sufficiency of organic matter, add some garden peat or well-rotted manure, or some compost. Work this in to a depth of 6 to 10 inches (15 to 25 cm). If the soil is too acid, add about 70 lb (31 kg) of chalk per 1000 sq ft (92 m²) of surface, depending on the degree of acidity (pH) shown by analysis.

Levelling the surface of the ground This task should normally be carried out before you do any digging-up or turning-over. Correct any uneven spots before you sow grass-seed. Fill in any depressions where water could gather, and remove any hummocks — these would be shaved bare when you mow the lawn.

Sowing The use of a spreader permits an even distribution which is more efficient and more economical in grass-seed. Divide your seed into two parts. Sow the first part up and down the lawn, and the other to and fro across. This will avoid any bare patches in the lawn.

Covering the seed and rolling lightly A leaf-rake of bamboo or steel (with long flexible teeth) is the ideal tool for covering the grass-seed with earth. The seed should be no more than half-buried in the soil, for it needs light to germinate. Avoid raking the seed into clumps. Then tamp lightly with an empty roller.

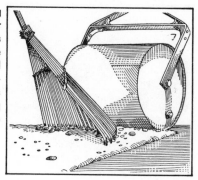

Fertilizing Spread a complete fertilizer — i.e., one which contains nitrogen, phosphorus and potassium (6-9-6, for example), in accordance with the instructions on the container. This fertilizing is done after the sowing, so that the nutritive elements are near the surface of the soil, where the first grass roots will be forming.

Watering Grass-seed must be kept moist, otherwise it will not germinate. Water very lightly with a fine drizzling spray, three times a day — at 10 a.m., 2 p.m., and 6 p.m. — unless there has been adequate rain that day. The first quarter-inch (0.7 cm) of the surface of the ground must be kept moist until all the seeds have sprouted.

Mowing Cut the lawn as soon as the grass is 3 inches (7.5 cm) high — cut it back to 2 inches (5 cm). Do not be alarmed if weeds appear here and there, as frequently happens. Before long the grass will have grown sufficiently thick and strong to choke off unwanted intruders.

Getting rid of weeds If weeds appear in the spring, get rid of them with a fertilizer containing weed-killer, or with a selective weed-killer. Follow the manufacturer's instructions closely.

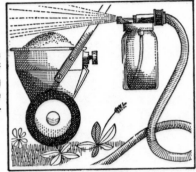

again two or three times, (as far too many people do) to produce an acceptable result — then you must buy the best seed available as far as quality and composition are concerned. Let me advise you as strongly as possible to ask advice of a seedsman or nurseryman of established reputation.

The new varieties of lawn grass which have come onto the market recently offer numerous advantages. As opposed to old-style grasses, these varieties are nearly all resistant to diseases. They are also more stocky and more bushy. They are left with more foliage after mowing. Also, they are more vigorous, last longer, resist weeds better and have a better appearance.

Types of seed

The best seed-mixtures for the Canadian climate are those which contain at least 70% fine permanent grasses, with Kentucky bluegrass and creeping red fescue each present in approximately equal amounts. The remaining 25% to 30% is made up of quick-growing grasses — white bent grass, creeping bent grass, fine bent grass and rye-grass — which protect the Kentucky bluegrass and the creeping red fescue and prevent weeds from getting the upper hand.

Sunny or shady locations

For a lawn on good garden soil, exposed to the sun or only lightly shaded, Kentucky bluegrass should predominate in the seed-mixture. In contrast, shady locations or on poorish soil, the proportion of fescue should be increased. Perennial rye-grasses are known for their rapid growth, which produces a fine-looking lawn with the minimum of delay. However, there should not be more than 15% to 20% of these grasses in the lawn-seed mxture, otherwise this could prove harmful to the bluegrasses which will find it difficult to stand up to such a high concentration of rye-grass. Bent grasses are excellent for dampish locations, and also on surfaces which will be kept cut very short.

Sowing the lawn

Here is the best method to follow for sowing a lawn. First of all, be quite sure as to the amount of seed to use: 4½ lb (2 kg) per 1000 sq ft (92 cm²) — which represents a plot of 20 x 50 ft (6 x 15 m); or 1 lb (0.45 kg) per 200 sq ft (18.5 m²) — which represents a plot 10 x 20 ft (3 x 6 m). After you have levelled the ground and rolled it, rake the surface lightly to break it up a little. To ensure an even distribution of the grass-seed, I suggest dividing the area to be sown into strips from 5 to 10 feet wide (choose whatever width suits you best), by means of parallel cords.

Levelling the ground is the first task to be done when you are laying out a lawn on a new property. Then spread a layer of soil of uniform texture and finally sow a grass-seed mixture, or lay sod.

Walk slowly down the first strip, then back up the second, and so on, sowing the seed as evenly as possible as you go. Use only **half** the total quantity of seed in this operation. Then remove the cords, rake the surface over lightly and replace the cords — but this time at right angles to their previous direction. Repeat the process and sow the other half of the seed, walking up and down the strips in the new direction. I recommend that you rake the surface again, then give it another light rolling. It is better not to pack the earth too tightly, so wear shoes without heels or lay a couple of planks underfoot during this operation.

Keep the seed-bed moist (but **not** flooded with water) until the grass is well established. To avoid washing the seed away, damp the soil down frequently with fine sprays of

If you must lay a lawn over a large area, it is better to call in a contractor who has the equipment to carry out large jobs.

short duration, rather than giving it a prolonged and heavy watering every now and then.

Laying a lawn on a steep slope or on a terrace presents some difficulties. Use mulches made from chopped straw, 1 to 2 inches (2.5 to 5 cm) thick. Alternatively, you could use a material loose enough to let the rain and the sunshine through while still preventing the seed from being washed away or scorched by the heat — such as sifted sphagnum moss, fibre or wood chips. Some people use peat-moss to cover their terraces. In general, however, there is no need to put mulch or sod on flat surfaces provided they are watered adequately when there is insufficient rainfall.

After the grass-seed has been sown uniformly with a spreader, rake the soil lightly with a lawn-rake to cover the seed.

The first mowing requires care

Seeds normally take two weeks to germinate. If the weather remains warm, you will need to cut the new grass — but not before it is at least 2 inches (5 cm) high. Adjust the blades of the mower to a cutting height of 1½ inches (4 cm). This first mowing is a delicate job which calls for some care, since it is all too easy to tear out the tender young grass which is not yet firmly rooted.

The best results are obtained with a reel-type mower — provided that the blades are properly sharp. If you must use a rotary mower, take care that it does not leave a mass of clippings which might stifle the new grass during the winter.

RENOVATING A LAWN

In the spring

It is easier than you might think to renovate an old lawn which has been neglected or invaded by crabgrass or other weeds. If this lawn contains at least 50% good lawn grass, more or less evenly distributed, then it can be renovated.

When you have to renovate a lawn partially or completely, and have decided to destroy part of the existing grass and weeds in order to lay a handsome new lawn, the easiest way to do this is to use a herbicide such as 'Weedrite' or 'Gramoxone' which will do the job in 24 hours. After that, you can create a new lawn — either by sowing seed or by covering the soil with strips of sod.

If there are areas covered with moss (which is usually attributable to poor soil, inadequate drainage or too much shade), spread some fertilizer over the affected area and improve the drainage if necessary. You could also use a product such as 'Moss Killer'.

However, if there are only a few small patches of good lawn-grass, there is only one solution — the whole lawn must be completely made over. While you are about it, take the opportunity of fertilizing the soil properly and improving the drainage.

Early in spring, as soon as the ground is free of snow and ice, clean off all the debris — branches, dead leaves, stones, etc. Use a rake with long flexible teeth for this.

Getting rid of dead grass

If the ground is covered with a thick layer of dead grass or culm, early spring is the ideal time to get rid of this harmful mulch which prevents air, water and nutritive elements from penetrating the soil down to the grass roots. For this task use either a grass rake, or motorized equipment, depending on the area that has to be dealt with. Many gardening centres will let you have the necessary equipment on a rental basis.

Fertilization carried out at the beginning of spring is extremely important — it might even be said that it is the most important of the whole season. As soon as the soil has dried out and become firm enough, feritlize it with a complete chemical fertilizer rich in nitrogen, such as 12-4-8, for example.

Aeration

I cannot stress too strongly how important it is to check the permeability of the soil of the lawn. To carry out this very simple little test, try to push a pencil into the soil to a depth of 4 inches (10 cm). If it is difficult to push it into the soil, then the soil is too hard-packed — with the result that

It is essential to rake the lawn in the spring to remove the culm or haulm (the layer of dead grass and clippings which forms on the surface and prevents air, water and fertilizer from reaching the roots of the grass).

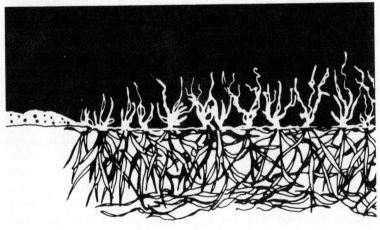

it is difficult, if not impossible, for water, air and nutritive elements to reach the roots. In this case, you must aerate the soil (i.e., make it more permeable). This can be done with a hand aerator, a motorized aerator (which you can rent from a gardening centre) or even with a garden fork if the area involved is very small. Some amateur gardeners use a lawn-roller fitted with aeration bars. Aeration can be carried out equally well in the autumn.

At the end of the summer

The end of the summer — from mid-August to mid-September — is the best time not only for laying a new lawn but also for renovating an existing one. During those four weeks, conditions of temperature and rainfall are most favourable for lawns of high-quality grass such as bluegrass, fescue and bent grass. Up until mid-September is the ideal time to lay a new lawn or renovate an existing one. The days are sunny and hot enough to warm up the soil, and the nights are cool — two factors that contribute to the rapid growth of vigorous lawn-grasses. Furthermore, weeds lose their strength at this time and are thus less danger to the grass. Finally, the conditions are most favourable for sowing — the soil is dry and easily worked — whereas in most cases it tends to be very wet in the spring-time.

Careful inspection

If an inspection of your lawn leads you to the conclusion that "something must be done", the first question to ask yourself is obviously — 'What?'

Essentially, there are three separate degrees of activity in the improvement and renovation of a lawn: improvement by a sound programme of maintenance; reseeding of an old lawn; or complete renovation. It is generally preferable to till a lawn, or dig it up and then relay it completely, if more than half the total surface area has been invaded by weeds.

However, if your lawn is not quite as 'jungly' as that, you could make do with a somewhat less radical programme.

As a start, let us examine the easiest method — improvement by a continuing programme of careful maintenance. Incidentally, you may be surprised to discover just how effective this method can be. First of all, you should cut the grass to its optimum height — 2 inches (5 cm) for Kentucky bluegrass, 1½ inches (4 cm) for 'Merion' bluegrass, and 1 inch (2.5 cm) for bent grass. If possible, do not let the grass clippings fall onto the lawn while you are mowing. Then rake the lawn vigorously with an all-purpose rake (provided with special teeth which make it easy to remove the culm) or with a bamboo or steel rake with long, flexible teeth. This raking will get rid of culm and other debris on the lawn. The piles of dead grass and other rubbish from the raking can then be swept up with a lawn-sweeper or sucked up by a garden vacuum machine. This treatment — removal of the culm, followed by sweeping or vacuuming — frees the grass and facilitates the penetration of air, water and fertilizers into the soil and down to the grass roots.

Few people have a lawn sufficiently large to warrant the purchase of a motorized rake for removing culm. Fortunately, many gardening centres nowadays keep this equipment, which is nevertheless essential for the production of a lovely lawn, and will rent it out at very reasonable prices.

However, before using this equipment, you would be advised to mow the lawn as short as possible and remove the grass clippings. You must also adjust the blades or teeth of the 'deculmer', so that the points only just penetrate the surface of the soil. All the culm is very soon removed and the lawn is then ready for the second operation — aeration.

Some lawns will not need to be aerated. For them, the shallow little furrows traced in the soil by the blades of the 'deculmer' are an ideal preparation for the seeding operation.

Aeration is essential

If the lawn has had to carry a lot of foot-traffic during the summer — as a site for games, perhaps, or a general meeting-place for the family — then its soil will have become hard-packed. Since aeration is essential, if your lawn is to remain healthy and vigorous, rent a motorized aerator at a gardening centre and perforate the entire lawn. The holes made by the aerator will allow air, water and fertilizers to penetrate into the soil.

In order to determine just how hard-packed the soil of the lawn really is, use the pencil test. Push a pencil down into the turf in several different places. If the pencil sinks in easily, then the soil is sufficiently porous. But if the opposite is true — i.e., if you have to push hard on the pencil to make it penetrate, then aeration is recommended. Aeration can also be carried out with a roller fitted with aeration bars, or with a small domestic aerator. It is better, however, to hire a motorized aerator — especially if you have never aerated the lawn before. If you are using an aerator that removes little carrot-shaped soil-cores, as opposed to merely making holes in the lawn, you must rake up all the little 'carrots', and fill in the bore-holes with good lawn soil.

Weeds

If the main problem is an invasion of weeds, use a weed-killer. You have a choice between granular and liquid products. When using chemical compounds of this nature, it is extremely important to follow the maker's recommendation to the letter.

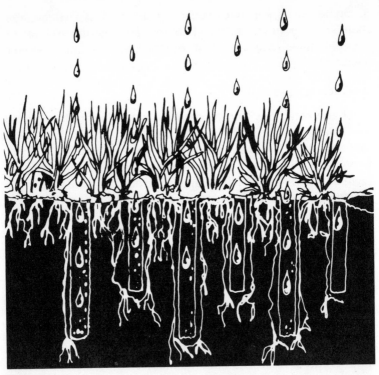

Aeration of the lawn may be carried out with a mechanical aerator, a garden fork, a spade, or any pointed instrument that will penetrate the culm and make an opening in the hardened soil. Air, water and nutritive elements can then enter the soil easily, and make their contribution to the vigorous growth of the lawn.

In addition, you should fertilize the lawn with a complete fertilizer — i.e., one which contains nitrogen, phosphorus and potassium. There are some fertilizers which also contain a weed-killer. Their use is becoming more popular since they allow you to fertilize the lawn and destroy the weeds in one single operation.

If you have a lawn with, say, more than 50% of its surface area occupied by weeds, I can only advise you to destroy the whole lawn with a non-selective weed-killer, then give the ground a thorough working-over with a rotary tiller or an ordinary hand-spade, depending on the surface area involved and the time at your disposal. Next, you must get rid of the clumps of old grass and level the surface with a rake or similar piece of equipment. Full preparation of the ground in this way will give you better results from your sowing than simpler renovation procedures. For example, it is impossible to mix a fertilizer into the soil properly unless the soil has been tilled right down to the level of the grass roots.

Getting the nutritive elements to penetrate deeply into the soil in this way is particularly important when the soil is packed, as is frequently the case in lawns with fairly heavy foot-traffic over them.

Bare patches

If your lawn consists of bluegrass, the bare patches left after getting rid of weeds will fill up rapidly. On the other hand, if the empty spaces are too large to be covered by the existing lawn-grass or if your lawn does not have enough high-quality grass in it, then you would do better to reseed those areas. First of all, loosen the soil of these bare patches, fertilize it, and lime it (if it is too acid). Then sow a mixture of high-quality grass seed (Canada No. 1) in the proportion of 1 lb (0.45 kg) per 1000 sq ft (92 m^2) of surface area. If it so happens that lawn-grasses are covering less than 30% of the surface, and the rest is either bare or covered with weeds, then you have no choice — the whole lawn must be completely relaid.

Relaying the lawn

If you must relay your lawn, either rent or borrow the necessary equipment to break up the turf and turn the under-lying soil over — a reto-tiller, or some similar piece of equipment. Loosen up the soil a little, level it, and then either sow seed or lay sod. If you are sowing, use 3 to 5 lb (1.3 to 2 kg) of grass-seed per 1000 sq ft (92 m²). You can work the seed into the soil with the back of a rake. Water with a very thin jet of water, or — better still — use a vaporizing spray.

The battle is only half-won

Once the seed has been sown, you might think that everything is all over and, with the help of the perfect temperatures as summer changes into autumn, the battle for the lawn has been won. However, success will only be achieved if you keep the seed surfaces damp. For a rapid, even growth, it is essential to water frequently so that the seeded areas are never allowed to dry out for long. In these circumstances, a mulch is of great value since it helps to preserve the moistness of the soil. Any material will do, so long as it allows the grass to grow up through it and preserves the humidity of the soil by cutting down evaporation. Straw is excellent, but it is not always easy to find. You can use ground horticultural peat, sphagnum moss or vegetable mould from a forest.

It is useless to expect good results without adequate fertilizing. The experts advise spreading about 25 lb (11 kg) of lawn-fertilizer per 1000 sq ft (92 m²) of surface area. A suitable formula is 6-9-6 — i.e., a complete fertilizer containing the three major fertilizing elements, nitrogen, phosphorus and potassium.

When the new grass appears, water it if the stems and leaves seem too limp. Adjust the blades of the lawn mower and cut the grass to a height of 1½ inches (4 cm) as soon as it is thick enough. Carry on cutting the new grass and sweep up the clippings each time so that when winter comes the grass will not be covered by a layer of accumulated culm. Lawns already established should continue to be cut regularly. The frequency of mowing is dictated by the rate of growth of the grass. However, you must always make sure never to remove more than a quarter, or at most a third, of the total leaf-surface of the lawn.

To those who prefer to lay sod rather than to sow seed, let me just say that while it is of course a quicker method, it is also more expensive. If you decide to use this method, you must make sure that you buy lawn turf of the highest possible quality, steering clear of prairie and pasturage grasses which contain mainly millet and clover and very often a high proportion of weeds as well.

Chapter IV

Fertilizing

FERTILIZING

At the beginning of the season, lawns are generally beginning to turn green, and are pleasing to the eye. But by mid-July the picture has changed considerably. Most lawns will have thinned out and bare patches will be in evidence — much to the despair of the gardener who, to the best of his knowledge, has taken all the necessary steps to keep his grass looking beautiful right through to autumn. How **does** one ensure that the lawn stays beautiful throughout the season?

What too many people forget about growing a lawn is that mowing it subjects the lawn-grasses to stress, and that these grasses have to survive in very artificial conditions. For example, if a bluegrass plant is allowed to grow naturally, it can cover a square foot (0.092 m^2) of soil and grow to a height of 24 to 36 inches (60 to 90 cm). In contrast, in a domestic lawn, forty plants or more are packed together into that area of one square foot. Furthermore, at regular intervals, the most active part of each plant is cut off by the lawn-mower, and this decreases its capacity to manufacture the nourishment which is essential for its survival.

Thus, something must be done to make amends. Without any doubt, fertilizing is one of the most important factors in the creation and maintenance of a fine lawn. I have had occasion to examine hundreds of lawns, with a view to discovering why the grass was not growing well. In the vast majority of cases — about 90% — the reason was that the grass was suffering from lack of nutrition.

Curiously enough, there is scarcely a single aspect of lawn maintenance that receives more attention than fertilizing. Unfortunately, the experts seem to concentrate mainly on insisting that **this** particular fertilizer should be used rather that **that** one, and hardly any attempt is made to give amateur gardeners a thorough grounding in the proper way to grow grass-plants. Every spring, thousands of bags

Fertilizing is one of the essential factors in the creation of a fine lawn.

of fertilizer are sold, and nearly all of them carry the statement: "The contents of this bag will fertilize 5000 sq ft (460 m²) of lawn". The amateur gardener quickly spreads the stuff over his lawn and heaves a sigh of relief, believing he has now given his grass everything it needs in the way of nutrition for the rest of the season.

It is perfectly true that a lawn may be fertilized quite successfully with 20 lb (9 kg) of 20-10-5 fertilizer. Even so, unless you give it three or four 'booster' treatments after the initial fertilizing in the spring, the lawn will be half-starved.

At each mowing the lawn loses a large amount of vegetable matter manufactured from mineral elements drawn from the soil. Thus, the stock of nutritive elements contained in the soil is very quickly depleted, and it is essential to build it up again if you wish to maintain a satisfactory rate of growth in the grass plants. You must therefore treat your lawn with fertilizers which will supply the grass-plants with the nourishment they need, in readily assimilable form. In addition, a proper fertilizing programme will do more to improve a poor lawn and keep a lovely one in good condition than almost any other measure.

Have the soil analyzed

If at all possible, it is a good idea to have your soil analyzed before you fertilize it. Any fertilizer you use on your lawn should contain nitrogen, to give it good growth and a rich green colour; phosphorus, for vigorous roots; and potassium, to give the plants resistance to diseases.

Chemical fertilizers should be bought for their quality and **not** for their low price-tag. In actual fact, their value depends on the total quantity of fertilizing elements contained in the bag and on the source of the nitrogen content of that particular fertilizer. If the fertilizer contains a slow-acting form of

Grass-seed will only take root where it can find fertilizer, or nutritive elements — not elsewhere. Poor and unproductive soil will hinder the growth of the roots.

nitrogen, the percentage of nitrogen insoluble in water will be shown on the label. If 35% or more of the total nitrogen content is guaranteed insoluble in water, you can be confident that you are buying a lawn fertilizer of good quality.

The ideal fertilizing programme for a lawn would allow the grass to grow at a uniform rate throughout the season. The nitrogen-containing materials in a fertilizer are certainly important when you are planning to set up a programme of this nature. These materials may be divided into two categories: those which release nitrogen quickly and those which release it slowly. Those in the first or "quick-release" group are soluble in water and immediately assimilable by the plants. The result is a sudden assimilation of the available nitrogen, followed by a slow loss over the next two to six weeks. To ensure a uniform growth-rate over a period of time, it is thus necessary to make frequent small "booster" applications of nutritive materials. In contrast, materials in the "slow-release" group, such as urea formaldehyde, are broken down by the micro-organisms in the soil to produce nitrogen in a form assimilable by the plants. A small quantity of nitrogen is thus being slowly but continuously released, over a very long period of time. This calls for applications at long intervals of time — which means less work for the gardener.

Using a spreader

Gardeners often complain that their lawns always grow unevenly. Many times, the uneven growth of the grass is quite simply due to inefficient spreading of the chemical fertilizer. The best way of tackling this job is to use a spreader.

With a good machine it is quite easy to regulate the flow with precision, and thus to follow the fertilizer manufacturer's recommendations to the letter. Furthermore, as the

For adequate fertilizing of your lawn, there is nothing to beat a spreader, which allows uniform distribution of the fertilizer.

spreader is pushed back and forth, it is possible to avoid putting too much fertilizer in some places and not enough in others.

Fertilizers containing weed-killers and pesticides

When May comes round, the soil begins to warm up and weeds begin to to grow — among them crabgrass. In many cases, ants, larvae, wireworms, whiteworms, lawn-moths, etc are getting ready to mount their summer attacks on your lawn. For a lawn infested with weeds (and in particular with crabgrass) and with its soil full of insect pests, there is only one solution if you want to have fine grass — and that is to use a special complete fertilizer, formula 12-4-8, which contains both herbicides and pesticides. In one operation you can fertilize your lawn and also get rid of weeds and insects.

To get the best results from this really marvellous fertilizer, it is important that it be spread during the first three weeks in May, before the lilacs and the apple-trees come into flower.

Before spreading it, mow the lawn, then rake away all organic debris (grass clippings, leaves, etc). Also, avoid using any organic cover-material such as horticultural peat at this time, since this could well spoil the effect of the special fertilizer. And finally, it is best spread on a sunny morning, and you should **not** water the lawn for the next three days.

Fertilizing in the summer

It sometimes happens that weeds reappear on the lawn in June. If this happens, the weeds can be rapidly eliminated by an application of the herbicide fertilizer 12-4-8.

Here too, it is advisable to pick a sunny morning for spreading the fertilizer, and once again you must neither mow nor water the lawn for the next three days.

If there are no weeds in the lawn, wait until July before fertilizing it, and then use an ordinary 12-4-8 fertilizer.

Fertilizing in July is also recommended in the case of lawns made from improved bluegrasses ('Merion', 'Fylking' etc), which need a really thorough fertilizing.

August is the perfect time to prevent the appearance of crabgrass in the following year. Use the special complete fertilizer, formula 12-4-8, containing herbicides (including a crabgrass-killer) and pesticides as well.

Fertilizing in the autumn

The final fertilization of the year should be cacrried out at the end of September. At that time, the grass is trying to build up a reserve of nutritive matter to get it through the winter and let it survive until the following spring, and especially to enable it to withstand the damages caused by snow-mould and ice. The recommended fertilizer on this occasion is 3-6-12.

SOME NOTES ABOUT CHEMICAL FERTILIZERS

MISCONCEPTIONS about chemical fertilizers

1. Chemical fertilizers are harmful to grass.
2. Chemical fertilizers should never be applied in warm weather.
3. A fertilizer provides all the nourishment needed by the lawn.
4. Every time you fertilize your lawn, you should use a complete fertilizer.
5. You should never use acid-forming fertilizers on lawns.

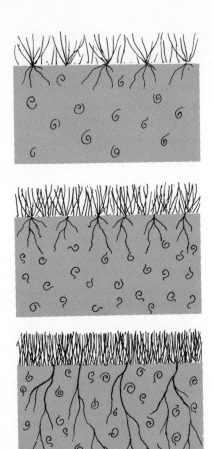

The top sketch shows a bare lawn: here, the grass-plants and the micro-organisms in the soil need nitrogen to make them healthy and vigorous. When nitrogen is added to the soil in the form of urea (see centre sketch), some of the micro-organisms transform it into ammonium salts. Other bacteria carry the nitrification process further, to produce nitrates — the only form in which nitrogen can be absorbed by grasses and other plants. Grass-plants (see bottom sketch) need a constant supply of nutritive elements if they are to develop a strong, healthy, vigorous root-system, as well as fine rich green stalks and blades. The soil itself benefits from the presence of the root-system, which increases its micro-organism content.

The TRUTH about chemical fertilizers

1. You can produce a fine lawn by using only a chemical or inorganic fertilizer, or an entirely organic fertilizer, or a fertilizer in the form of urea, or a mixture of all these types — povided only that you use them properly.

2. Heavy applications of fertilizer should always be made in the spring, but light applications made in the summer are sometimes very useful. Summer applications of nitrogen improve the colour of the grass and prevent 'Merion' bluegrass rust. However, the summer is not really the best time to fertilize thinly-sown lawns which have crabgrass and other summer weeds in them.

3. As for other plants, the basic nourishment of the grasses is carbohydrate, produced by the process of photosynthesis — the action of the sun on the chlorophyl in the individual blades. What fertilizers provide, with the help of the soil and its constituent elements, is the minerals required for the formation of more complex compounds and for numerous biological processes.

4. The soil can retain large quantities of phosphorus and potassium. If it has built up a good stock of these elements it may well be that nitrogen is the only fertilizing element required for several years. Nitrogen is exhausted rapidly and must be replaced as required.

5. Most of the products used to provide lawns with nitrogen are acid-forming. The exceptions are sodium nitrate and calcium cyanamide, which are rarely used. The commonest chemical fertilizers (which use ammonium nitrate) and natural organic products containing urea (either pure or in other forms) generally have much the same effect on the acidity of the soil. Any acidity caused by nitrogen-rich fertilizers can easily be neutralized with lime.

Chapter V

Maintenance of the Lawn

Just like flowerbeds and the kitchen-garden, your lawn needs certain basic attentions if it to show good results. For example, you must prepare the soil before sowing seed — just as you would for the rest of the garden.

A beautiful lawn is the result of constant and attentive care. Too many people imagine that once the seed has been sown, or the sod laid, all they have to do thereafter is water it and mow it from time to time — and that will create and maintain a lovely carpet of greenery which will send the neighbours wild with jealousy. A pipe-dream, of course — nothing could be further from the truth.

For normal growth, grass requires the addition of nutritive elements, as well as the elimination of weeds which often engage the grass-plants in a bitter struggle for the available space, nourishment and water.

Insect pests and plant diseases must be tracked down and controlled before they do too much damage. In addition, just like trees, shrubs and vegetables, lawn-grass needs water. The essential difference between the lawn and the rest of the garden is that the former involves dealing with a solid mass or strong concentration of plants, rather than with individual or isolated plants as is the case with flower-beds and borders. From that very fact, the horticultural methods required in the two cases are completely different.

IN THE SPRING

If you want to be really proud of your lawn during the coming summer, you must get down to the preliminary tasks of lawn-maintenance as early as possible in the spring.

The very first task in the maintenance of a lawn comes early in the spring-time — i.e., in April, as soon as the snow has melted and the ground has firmed up enough: it consists of immediately removing all the debris — bits of wood, and

Guide to a good lawn

1. Underneath trees and in spots which are hard to get at, it is preferable to plant carpeting plants rather than grass.
2. Carefully sweep up all dead leaves and other debris.
3. An edge-cutter is very useful for cutting the grass near the edges, and along walls.
4. Water long enough to let the water penetrate deeply into the soil.
5. The spreader is the thing to use to fertilize your lawn efficiently.
6. Keep your mower in good running order, so that it cuts the lawn uniformly.
7. Replace any bare patches in the lawn.
8. Aeration of the soil allows air, water and fertilizer to penetrate into the soil and reach the grass roots.
9. Jute screens protect newly-sown areas.
10. Long grass should be scythed.
11. Bamboo or steel rakes with long flexible teeth will remove dead leaves and other debris without damaging the grass.
12. Weeds should be removed with weed-killers — or if there are only a few of them, you can lift them out with a dandelion-spud.
13. Fungi are caused by the presence of rotting wood or other organic material in the soil. Remove the cause, and the fungus itself will quickly disappear.
14. Keeping the borders of your flowerbeds neat and tidy is easier if you use a pair of lawn clippers and some plastic or metal edging.

stones, etc, and all the dead leaves scattered over the surface of the lawn. Use a rake with long, flexible teeth for this job. Then fertilize the lawn without delay, since the grass-plants are hungry after the long winter months.

Removing dead grass

The dead grass which covers the surface of the soil is called the 'culm'. It prevents water and the nutritive elements

Problems inherent in a lawn (1) During the dry spells which occur during the hottest part of the summer, it may happen that the grass in certain areas of your lawn takes on a dull blue-gray colour, alternatively, it may go yellowish. You must then adjust your mower so that it cuts less closely. (2) A yellowish tinge and a slowing-down in growth indicate that the lawn needs fertilizing. Bluish-gray grass indicates lack of water. The lawn should be watered long enough to let the water penetrate 6 inches (15 cm) into the soil. (3) Patches of dead grass may be encountered, damp, and grey-brown in colour, with clearly-defined borders. (4) Lift the turf at the affected areas, and you will find the larvae which are at the root of the problem.

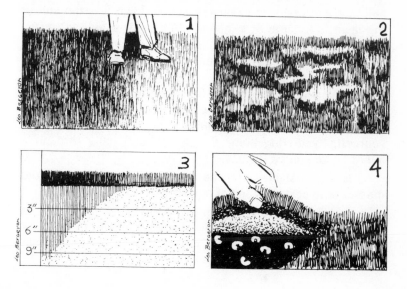

of fertilizers from getting down to the grass roots and it must be removed without delay. To get rid of this dead grass, use a special 'deculming' rake. If you are dealing with large areas, it would be better to rent a motorized 'deculmer' from a gardening centre. You will be surprised by the quantity of cum you will collect in this way.

Rolling

I would advise you to roll the lawn at the beginning of the season, to push down the tufts of grass which were forced up during the winter by the action of frost followed by thaw. Rolling also flattens out the tiny hillocks made by earth-worms. However, if your soil is at all hard-packed — especially if you have a clayey soil — you would be wiser **not** to pack it even harder by using a heavy roller on it.

Aerating the soil

Here is a little trick to let you test the firmness of the soil. Early in May, try to push a pencil down into the soil of the lawn to a depth of 4 inches (10 cm). If it will not go in, the soil is too hard-packed — which in turn means that most of the water and nutritive elements cannot get down to the grass roots. All you need to do to correct this failing is to aerate the soil. There are motorized aerators which resemble the machines used on golf courses, available for rent at garden centres. It is also quite easy to make an aerator yourself, by driving some 6-inch (15 cm) nails through a board 1 foot square (0.092 m^2).

It is also possible to buy aeration bars which can be fitted quickly onto certain types of lawn roller.

I cannot stress too strongly how essential aeration is in the creation of a perfect lawn. The work need not be done only in the spring-time, it is also of importance to aerate the lawn in the autumn.

Removal of the culm or haulm, the layer of dead grass at the roots, is an essential operation in the maintenance of a lawn. It is possible to rent motorized equipment at gardening centres, which will make this task considerably easier.

Fertilizing

Do not waste any time after you have cleaned, deculmed and aerated the lawn. Get on with the job of fertilizing it straight away. Incidentally, this first treatment of the season is the most important. It will have a decisive influence on the quality of the grass throughout the summer.

You should use a complete chemical fertilizer which will not burn the grass and which contains the three major nutri-

The lawn-aerator is the ideal piece of equipment for aerating your lawn and keeping it in good condition. The results produced in close-packed soil make it possible for air, water and nutritive elements to reach the grass roots.

tive elements — nitrogen, phosphorus and potassium in the proportions 3-1-2 — as well as some special minerals.

In addition, the nitrogen must be in a form in which it can nourish the grass-plants quickly at the start, and then keep them fertilized for several weeks thereafter. The fertilization formula most generally recommended and used is 12-4-8. This is also the most popular formula for golf courses and the grass in public parks.

A treatment like this helps the grass resist dryness and gives it a lovely green colour which it will retain for a long time.

The motorized aerator is perfect for aerating the larger lawns. This piece of equipment may be rented at most gardening centres.

Brown spots

It often happens that a lawn goes bare in patches where the grass has disappeared as a result of frost, ice, fungus diseases or insect pests. These bare patches are quite easily restored. All you have to do is remove the dead grass, turn the soil over with a spade, then sow the bare patch with good-quality grass-seed, or lay sod over it.

These brown spots are not always attributable to cryptogamic diseases (which are caused by microscopic fungi). Very often they are due to excessive composting. dead leaves or pieces of wood or other objects which have been left too long in the same place. Dogs and heaps of grass clippings are also frequently responsible for these nasty brown patches. They may also be caused by herbicides, fertilizers applied when the grass was wet, fungicides, over-fertilization, oil or gasoline from the lawn-mower, or by insecticides.

In addition, certain larvae — such as those of the Japanese bettle or the June-bug — are responsible for some brown spots.

IN THE SUMMER

I canot stress too strongly that a beautiful lawn forms the crowning jewel of a beautiful property. Even though growing lawn-grass is relatively less complicated than growing other plants — herbaceous perennials and annuals, for example, as well as woody plants — nevertheless a lawn worthy of the name cannot be obtained without taking pains. You must not think that once you have sown your seed or laid your sod all your problems are over, and all you have to do is sit back and admire the results of your labours. Even if you have used a first-class lawn seed containing Kentucky bluegrass, bent grass, fescue and rye-grass in the proportions recommended by all the gardening experts, or have laid high-quality sod on your lawn — that is merely the beginning — at the most, a good beginning.

The 'Cyclone'-type spreader is the perfect piece of equipment for reseeding a lawn that has become somewhat bare.

Requirements for maintaining a lawn in good condition

Remember that in a well-kept lawn the individual blades of grass must be kept constantly clipped to a uniform height and tightly packed against each other. Although they are crowded together in this way, the grass-plants must be kept in good health by a programme of plentiful fertilizing, adequate watering, rigorous control of insect pests, etc. In contrast with the grass that grows wild in the fields, alongside roads or on waste ground, lawn grass-plants have to undergo conditions so severe that if the careful attention required by these conditions is relaxed for even a few weeks, the grass deteriorates considerably. The **sine qua non** in the maintenance of a lawn of which you can be proud is constant care. It should be stressed that dwarf plants — which include grass-plants — do not have the reserves of nutritive elements or the depth of root which would allow them to survive during periods of dryness or serious attacks by disease.

An element of beauty

Although a truly decorative lawn requires a great deal of care, it is really worth the trouble — for it forms the basic element in any successful landscaping plan. With the methods, products and equipment that modern techniques have made available to amateur gardeners, it is relatively

A small portable seeder. This piece of equipment, which is adjustable, is very useful for broadcast sowing on areas which are hard to get at and it avoids the wastage that accompanies hand-sowing. It may also be used for spreading granular fertilizer.

easy to produce a lawn to be proud of. Everything needed for success is there, within easy reach of anyone who wants to make use of it. For example, there are precision spreaders for seeds, fertilizers and manures; sprinkler systems, automatic sprayers, new herbicides and fungicides and so on, and on.

With the arrival of the first warm weather of the spring, amateur gardeners can scarcely control their enthusiasm. They are impatient to get to work on their land, to start caring for their plants — and above all to get the lawn into shape. But when summer comes along, they begin hearing the call of the mountains or the sea, or they are smitten with the urge to play golf or go on fishing-trips, and all too many of them find their enthusiasm waning considerably, if not completely, so the maintenance of the lawn is put off until the autumn or even the following spring. If the grass grows too high, all its gets is a hasty cut every now and then. Inevitably such negligence during the summer months creates problems which are often difficult to solve, for what a handsome lawn needs most of all is appropriate and adequate care during the summer season.

Many factors influence the appearance of a lawn. First and foremost, I would say, is the quantity of water it receives, either naturally through rain or artificially, through watering.

Other important factors include the compactness of the surface of the soil, drainage, frequency of mowing and height of the cut, the level of fertility of the soil and the presence of weeds, insect pests and diseases.

A minimum of work

In normal conditions, it should be possible to produce a good lawn in most parts of Canada and to make it last — provided that you use guaranteed grass-seed or strips of

What could be more pleasant than lying out on a handsome lawn, on a beautiful sunny day? However, a fine carpet of greenery demands a great deal of careful attention. Nothing must be neglected — aeration, removal of culm, watering, fertilizing, doing battle with insects and diseases, and so on.

high-quality sod, and that you have prepared the ground properly and are using the appropriate methods of maintenance.

If you give your lawn the necessary care in the springtime — such as cleaning, rolling, fertilizing, removing the culm, and reseeding if necessary — then maintenance work during the summer will be reduced to a minimum and will consist mainly of mowing, watering, fertilizing and possibly dealing with crabgrass.

Most lawn problems can be eliminated by a suitable mowing and a treatment with a nitrogen-rich fertilizer, for these two measures encourage the vigorous growth of the grass while at the same time killing off clover and other weeds.

VARIOUS CHORES

Raking

When using a rake after mowing the lawn, all you should do is remove the surplus clippings which are lying on top of the blades of grass and which might stifle them. Never rake a lawn hard enough to remove **all** the clippings.

Rolling

I would advise you to roll the lawn to make sure that the grass-seed penetrates the soil, or to push down any clumps of grass which have come loose at the roots during the winter. However, you should **not** use a roller with the idea of improving the level of the ground — although a rolling in the spring is recommended if there has been any "heaving" due to frost.

Composting

This is a common way of rejuvenating a lawn that has become old and mangy to a greater or lesser degree, or of restoring grass where weeds have left bare spots after being killed off by weed-killers. Every two years, in August, spread humus or some organic matter such as peat-moss or compost, enriched with 'Milorganite' or a nitrogen-rich fertilizer in the proportions of 5 lb (2 kg) per 1000 sq ft (92 m^2) of surface area. A layer $\frac{1}{4}$ to $\frac{1}{2}$ inch (0.6 to 1.5 cm) thick is sufficient for this application. Then work this organic matter into the ground with a bamboo rake, the object being to cover the roots of the grass-plants rather than the leaves.

Weed-killers

Wherever there is a lawn weeds will always be a problem. The seeds of weeds are usually present in the soil before any grass-seed is sown. Furthermore, if you have created your lawn by sodding it with pasturage sod, you should not

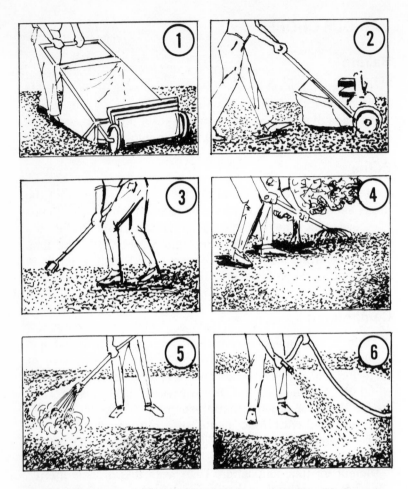

A fine-looking lawn calls for the appropriate attention (1) Sweeping removes grass-clippings. (2) Mowing should be done with a mower with properly-sharpened blade or blades. (3) An edge-cutter or trimmer is indispensable for cutting the grass properly along walls, borders, flowerbeds, etc. (4) An all-purpose rake, or a scarifier with well-sharpened teeth, will remove the culm stifling the grass roots at the surface of the soil. (5) Dead leaves and other debris are removed from the lawn with a rake with flexible teeth. (6) Watering provides lawn-grasses with the water they require for normal growth.

A dense, velvety lawn shows the importance of high-quality lawn-grasses, adequately fertilized and regularly watered, and of careful mowing.

be surprised when you notice patches of coarse and undesirable grass in it. To avoid this unfortunate result, buy turf only from a nurseryman or seedsman of good reputation.

Spreading manure, or manure-enriched loam on the surface of your lawn is not recommended because of the risk of spreading seeds of weeds which may be in the manure at the same time.

It is quite possible to kill off most weeds in a lawn by practising growth methods which will ensure a dense and vigorous growth of grass-plants, and by an appropriate use of weed-killers. For broad-leaved weeds such as the dandelion and the plantain, apply a 2,4-D amine at the moment when the weeds are at the peak of their growth.

Some weeds — such as chickweed — will prove harder to kill off. Treat these with 'Silvex' or 'Mecoprop', or a mixture of the two, with or without a 2,4-D amine. Against crabgrass you should use 'Dacthal', 'Trifluraline' or 'Zytron', at the end of May or the beginning of June. In all cases, it is highly important that you should use these preparations in strict accordance with the instructions on the container.

Weed-killers should be sprayed onto the lawn on a windless day, to avoid damage to nearby shrubs and ornamental plants. In addition, you should give the sprayer a thorough cleaning with a detergent solution before you use it again for some other anti-pest preparation.

Grass has other enemies beside weeds. The earthworm is a typical example, but these can be destroyed by using lead arsenate. 'Chlordane' is a good all-purpose pesticide for use against whiteworms, ants and other insects.

Sowing seed

Grass-seed is sown when it becomes necessary to replace grass in spots where weeds have left bare patches after being killed by an application of weed-killer, to replace grass destroyed by fungus diseases or with the object of rejuvenating an old lawn. Sowing should be followed by a light rolling.

Water the surface once it has been sown, and keep it moist until the new shoots of grass make their appearance. Take care to water only with a very fine spray of water which will neither pack the surface soil nor wash the seed away. If the first watering saturates the soil, subsequent waterings can be very light (though they should be frequent). These will be sufficient until the seed germinates.

Chapter VI

Mowing and Watering

Kentucky bluegrass and fescue cut to ground level will give you only a shallow-rooted lawn that will need watering every day.

2" CUT

Kentucky bluegrass and fescue will spread by reproduction of their roots beneath the surface. to form a deeply-rooted and extremely thick lawn — provided they are not cut too short.

1" CUT

All lawn-grasses need sun. So called special 'shade' grasses last only a little longer in the shade than other types of grass.

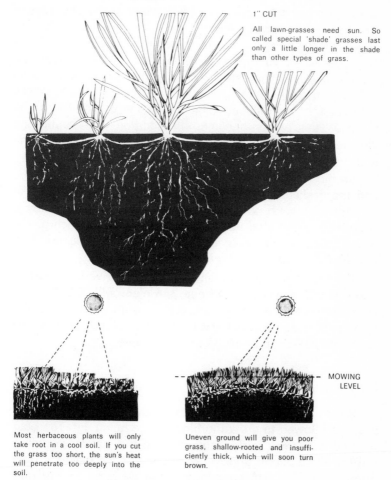

MOWING LEVEL

Most herbaceous plants will only take root in a cool soil. If you cut the grass too short, the sun's heat will penetrate too deeply into the soil.

Uneven ground will give you poor grass, shallow-rooted and insufficiently thick, which will soon turn brown.

MOWING THE LAWN

A lovely lawn can easily be destroyed in one single season as a result of faulty mowing practices which weaken the root-system of the lawn-grasses and prevent them from recovering their vigour after each mowing.

Many people believe that mowing the lawn is good for the grass. Yet it is common knowledge that the real reason for mowing the lawn is, quite simply, to improve its appearance. Furthermore, the necessary nourishment for the grass is produced above the level of the soil, in the leaves, by means of photosynthesis — i.e., by the action of the sunlight — therefore, the more foliage there is, the more nourishment is produced (and hence more roots) and the stronger the plants become. In addition, the depth and vigour of the roots are almost exactly proportional to the above-ground height of the grass.

As the grass-plant grows higher, its base becomes more and more shaded, and more bleached-looking. This part of the foliage lacks chorophyll, and is therefore unable to manufacture the vital nutritive elements. If too much of the grass blade is cut off in one single mowing, you are also getting rid of too much chlorophyll.

The result is that the plant becomes deprived of nourishment. If this happens only once, the plant will not die from it — although it is weakened, the roots in particular being affected. On the other hand, if it happens several times during the same season, the results are disastrous.

Mow frequently

What I have just described is exactly what happens if the grass is allowed to grow too high before being cut. The best method is to mow fairly frequently, so that not more than a third of the blade of grass is removed at each mowing. How often should you cut your lawn? That depends on the rate

Once the grass has been mown, the clippings MUST be removed. They are damp and heavy, and if allowed to remain they will stifle the grass and destroy its roots.

Heavy mowers crush the soil and squeeze out the air which the roots need if they are to survive. The grass becomes thin, and loses its resistance.

Mowing restores freshness to the grass by removing broken blades. Badly-sharpened mowers fray the tips of the blades, the grass loses its lustre, and turns brown.

Chemical products supposed to inhibit the growth of weeds often merely hinder the growth of the grass. The weeds seize their opportunity, and move in on the weakened grass.

Before mowing the lawn, you must remove all the debris and clutter.

of growth. A lawn consisting mainly of Kentucky bluegrass will need cutting twice as frequently during the spring-time as it will during the summer or the autumn.

If you do not cut your grass frequently enough, with the result that it grows too tall, do **not** cut it back completely in one single mowing. Remove only so much as will still leave enough chlorophyll in the plants, and cut the grass back gradually, over several mowings, until you have got it down to the proper height.

The height of the cut

Regular and systematic mowing during the summer is an operation that should not be neglected. The height of the cut depends on many factors, such as the kinds of grass in the lawn, the climatic conditions and the planned future use of the lawn (e.g., games or sitting-out). For example, 'Merion' bluegrass, an improved variety of Kentucky bluegrass, may be cut much shorter than the latter.

Mowing the lawn is an operation that calls for the greatest of care — if you want to have a lovely lawn. A well-executed cut reinforces the root-system of the lawn-grasses and renews their vigour. You must adjust your mower so that it cuts to a height of 1½ to 2 inches (4 to 5 cm). This is the best height, and also the safest.

A dense, well-fertilized grass can usually be cut more frequently than a thin grass lacking in fertilizing elements. A low cut, systematically repeated, encourages the lateral growth of the grass-plants, thus helping to produce a lawn which is compact and therefore easier to maintain. A low cut also helps to control broad-leaved weeds.

Most grasses used in lawn-seed mixtures grow better if you cut them to a height of 1½ to 2 inches (4 to 5 cm). A lawn trimmed to 1½ inches (4 cm) is less subject to diseases, winter damage and stifling than a lawn cut to a height of 2½ inches (6 cm). You should start mowing your lawn in the spring-time and carry on through to the autumn, as long as the grass continues to grow.

The thickness of grass removed in any single mowing should never exceed 1½ inches (4 cm). Thus, in spring, the lawn will need cutting twice a week, but only once a week a little later on.

For a high-quality grass (a mixture containing Kentucky bluegrass, bent grass, fescue and rye-grass, or any other suitable mixture), adjust the height of the blades or reel of your mower to 1½ inches (4 cm) both in the spring-time and in the autumn. During the really hot summer weather, the grass should not be cut shorter than 2 inches (5 cm).

New grass should be cut before it grows so long that it cannot stand upright. It can be cut as soon as it has reached a height of about 2½ inches (6 cm).

In addition, recent experiments have shown that too low a cut is seriously detrimental to the growth of the grass roots.

It is not a good idea to leave the grass long in the autumn. This practice brings severe disadvantages in its wake. The blades of grass are crushed together under their own weight, or as a result of heavy rain, or under the snow, and this encourages the incidence of snow-mould. If the grass is mown at regular intervals, before it gets too long, you can leave the clippings on the lawn. They will disappear rapidly and also nourish the grass as they rot. The most important thing is **not** to let the grass grow to a height of 3 to 4 inches (7.5 to 10 cm) and then cut it back to 1½ to 2 inches (4 to 5 cm) at one time.

The reel or blades of your lawn-mower must be properly sharp in order to give a good clean cut. If you allow your mower to get blunt, the ends of the individual blades of grass are mangled and the lawn takes on a browninsh tinge. With a new lawn made from young grass a blunt mower may simply tear the grass out of the ground.

You should also bear in mind that reel-type mowers give a better cut than rotary mowers.

The truth about mowing

The maintenance of lawns is one of the favourite subjects of gardening experts who write in countless magazines and newspapers. Unfortunately, some of their articles are not too clear and sometimes they are even completely and utterly incorrect. Home-owners who are anxious to improve their lawns, but who know little or nothing about the subject, are all too easily impressed by these fallacious articles. Here are some very prevalent misconceptions about lawn-mowing, followed by the true facts of the matter:

Five MISCONCEPTIONS about mowing

1. Cutting the grass short means that the lawn may be mown less frequently.
2. Raking up the grass clippings damages the lawn.
3. Close cuts in spring encourage the grass to spread.
4. Cutting the grass short stops weeds coming to seed and thus reduces the problems they pose.
5. Letting the grass grow long to face the winter helps it to survive.

Five TRUTHS about mowing

1. Grass that has been cut too short grows less than grass cut to the proper height — 1½ to 2 inches (4 to 5 cm) — but it still needs cutting just as often. The right time to mow is dictated by the untidy look of shaggy grass. Experiments have shown that grass cut to a height of ¾ inch (2 cm) needs cutting just as often as grass cut to 2 inches (5 cm).
2. A thinly-sown lawn which has not been suitably fertilized can benefit from the clippings being left where they lie. On the other hand, a thickish and well-fertilized lawn always looks better, and is generally in a better condition, if the clippings are raked up — though this does not mean to say it is impossible to have a handsome lawn without removing the clippings. Often the improved appearance is not worth the trouble it takes to rake up the clippings.

A well-executed mowing leaves the lawn looking like a handsome green carpet.

3. The shorter the grass is cut, the more harm done. There is no doubt that the vigour of the grass depends on the area of the leaves exposed to the sun.

4. Some weeds cannot survive short cuts, but others do, quite easily — even if they are cut lower than the average mowing height. Crabgrass, and many other weeds will produce seeds even if they are cut back to 3/16 or ¼ inch (0.5 to 1 cm). Also, experiments have shown that Kentucky bluegrass cut to a height of 1 inch (2.5 cm) produces twenty times more seed than if cut to ¼ inch (1 cm).

5. Winter rarely kills off perennial lawn grasses such as Kentucky bluegrass, fescues or the other "cool-weather" types. However, if the grass is too long when winter sets in, it is more subject to diseases such as snow-mould. The proper practice is to go on cutting the grass until it stops growing in the autumn.

WATERING

To keep your lawn beautifully green and attractive all the time, you must water it all summer. It needs watering every time inspection of the soil shows it to be dry to a depth of more than ½ inch (1.5 cm), or if the grass is starting to take on a bluish tint which shows it is beginning to wilt. Let me advise you to water often enough, and in sufficient quantity each time, to make sure that the deeper layers of the soil never get completely dried out. On the other hand, you should never water the soil to the point where it is completely soaked all the time. Also, when watering a lawn, never forget that different soils have different structures.

The water in the soil

This is one of the most important factors in the growth of grass. Nutritive elements may be available in the soil, but without water they can neither dissolve nor be assimilated by the plant — and this of course slows down growth

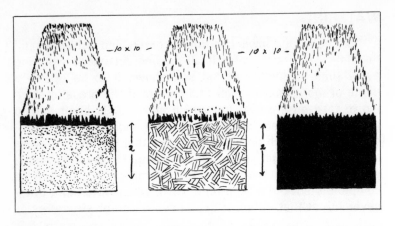

Water-absorption capacity of different types of soil. On the left, sandy soil — 60 gallons (270 l); in the centre, vegetable soil — 90 gallons (405 l); on the right, clayey soil — 160 gallons (720 l).

completely. It is water which gives the plant its upright stance; if there is no water, the plant just wilts and withers away.

Relationship between the water and the soil

Water exists within the soil in three separate forms:

Hygroscopic water: this water cannot be used by grass-plants because it is too firmly held within the particles of the soil. It can only be released by baking the soil in an oven.

Gravitational water: this is water which trickles downward in the soil under the force of gravity. It fills the relatively large spaces between the particles of the soil and drives the oxygen out. We say then that the soil is "saturated". As gravitational water drains through the soil, it leaches out some of the nutritive elements and also entrains pure, fresh air. Plants make use of gravitational water.

Capillary water: this is the form of water most used by the plants. It fills the spaces between the particles of the soil and remains suspended around individual particles in the form of an unbroken film held there by surface tension. This water mixes with the air in the soil. The amount of capillary water in the soil lies between these two limits:

1 — The field capacity: this describes the maximum quantity of capillary (or usable) water that the soil can hold.

2 — The dry-out point: this describes the situation where capillary water is no longer available to the plant.

Coarse-textured soils, with large spaces between the particles (such as sand), drain well and allow air to circulate freely. However, they have poor water-retention capacity. Fine-textured soils (such as clay, silt and loam) have small spaces between the particles but a large internal surface area; they retain water more easily, but they are difficult to aerate, and they drain more slowly.

This type of oscillating sprinkler (which is completely adjustable) covers up to 2400 sq ft (220 m²) of lawn. It also has the advantage that it works effectively even when the water-pressure is low.

An automatic irrigation system gives uniform watering, and distributes the water over the whole surface of the lawn.

How the water rises in the soil

Capillary water forms a thin film around the individual particles of the soil by means of surface tension. During its growth process, the plant "breathes" and loses water though the surface of its leaves. This creates a space which exerts a strong tractive or tensile force running down from the leaf toward the stem and the roots, into the soil, and so to the spaces between the particles with their films of water. This tensile force draws the water upward toward the plant and the upward movement continues, with the film of water becoming thinner and thinner, until the point is reached where the tensile force exerted by the soil particles is equivalent to that exerted by the plant. Then the upward movement of the water ceases. The dry-out point has been reached, and the plant begins to die.

RAIN

In most regions of Canada, there is enough rainfall to make the grass grow, but this rainfall is not equally distributed throughout the year.

During heavy storms, almost all the water runs off without benefitting the plants; while during hot, dry spells there is not enough rain to provide all the water needed. Therefore, gardeners must resort to artificial watering.

Watering
The key to success

A lawn must be well watered — i.e., until the water penetrates 3 to 4 inches (7.5 to 10 cm) below the surface. Most of the grasses which go to make up a lawn need 1 inch (2.5 cm) of water per week. If rainfall does not provide this amount of water, as is usually the case during the summer, artificial means become necessary. The key to success when watering a lawn is to saturate it with water, as opposed to merely sprinkling it. Frequent but superficial watering is not the right answer, and can even be harmful by causing the roots to bunch up near the surface so that they dry out during the summer.

The most successful method is a copious watering which penetrates several inches into the surface of the ground, performed once or twice a week during hot, dry periods. This operation can be carried out with an ordinary sprinkler which you move about on the lawn at half-hour intervals.

Keeping your lawn a lovely uniform shade of green throughout the summer calls for a programme of watering tailored to fit the requirements of the grass. Although it is not a very arduous task, using modern equipment, there can be no doubt that watering is still an absolutely essential factor for successful gardening.

In most soils, the grass roots go down two feet and more — unless they are hampered by lack of humidity or by the compactness of the soil. The roots will not penetrate a dry soil, or one that is so badly drained that lack of oxygen hinders the normal growth of the plants.

Although most of the water used for watering will contain various chemical products (chlorine, alum, etc), the rain will wash away the more toxic chemical compounds. You can use your local water-supply without fear of damage from chemical products, unless there is something very obviously wrong that calls for a proper laboratory analysis.

A question of judgement

Watering must be carried out with judgement. In the first place, you should ensure that your grass plants have deep roots so that they retain water as long as possible. The humidity of the soil is a factor of prime importance in the maintenance of a beautiful green lawn. When the temperature and the state of the soil show that the lawn lacks moisture, you must water it until the soil is thoroughly damp down to a depth of 3 or 4 inches (7.5 to 10 cm) below the surface. Watering like this helps the grass-plants to extend their roots deeply. If you want to know when to water your lawn, dig a narrow hole — with an auger, for example — 3 or 4 inches (7.5 to 10 cm) down into the soil. If the soil is dry near the surface, you should water it until it is moist to a depth of 3 or 4 inches (7.5 to 10 cm).

Water the lawn until the water begins trickling over the surface, then stop watering for a moment or two, and then begin again. Go on doing this until the soil is damp to the full depth required.

A few hours devoted to the care of your grass during summer will give you a magnificent lawn that will form a background of rich green velvet for your flowers and your house.

When to water

Water the lawn before the grass begins to show that it is necessary. The first sign is loss of elasticity. For example, your footprint remains visible in the grass after you have moved on. If the grass is not watered immediately, it will begin to turn brown.

The best time for watering is in the early evening, when the air temperature is beginning to drop. That cools the grass and the soil down a little and helps produce more dew. If the grass is being dried out by too much warm, dry weather, then you must water it in the middle of the day to lower its temperature. The blades of grass will soon return to their normal condition then.

The practice of leaving a sprinkler on all night must be condemned out of hand. This procedure is very harmful to a lawn, since the resulting excess of water encourages the incidence of fungus diseases.

If there are trees and bushes competing with the lawn for the available water, then obviously some extra ration will have to be supplied A Norwegian maple can evaporate as much as 150 gallons (675 l) of water a day — which is equivalent to the loss of 3 quarts of water per square foot (3.4 l per 929 cm²). Thus, lawns which lie beneath large trees may need up to 1 gallon of water per square foot (4.5 l per 929 cm²) per day during really hot weather.

The rate of watering

Never water faster than the absorption capacity of the ground will permit. If water starts trickling over the surface of the ground before the soil is saturated to the proper depth, then that water is being lost almost as fast as you are pouring it on. It is likely to cause erosion, too, or to leach out the fertilizing elements. This is the sort of situation you see very frequently on slopes, such as embankments.

Water slowly, until the soil is dampened right down to the very bottom level of the root-system — i.e., from 8 to 12 inches (20 to 35 cm). Then wait until that water has been used up before you carry out another watering.

Another method of watering consists of supplying only half the necessary water, then repeating the operation a few hours later. This method keeps the root-system in excellent shape, and very active.

The type of soil

Do not forget that the composition of the soil determines the quantity of water required. A heavy, clayey soil can be saturated quite easily, but the water soaks into it slowly. On the other hand, a sandy soil will absorb water almost as fast as you choose to pour it on. So it is important to know what sort of soil you have. You must also know its water-absorption capacity — which indicates how long you must wait before you can apply more water without causing it to trickle over the surface of the soil. Each type of soil also has its own water-retention capacity. The larger the soil particles, the less time water is retained. Thus, a block of sandy soil 10 feet square (3 x 3 m) by 2 feet deep (0.6 m) can only hold 120 gallons (540 l) of water; whereas a block of clayey soil of the same size can retain 320 gallons (1440 l).

The quantity of water

Several methods can be used to measure the quantity of water delivered to the lawn. The simplest is to stand a series of empty tin cans at strategic spots over the area. Since these cans have parallel vertical sides, the amount of water they collect gives you a reasonably accurate picture of the quantity of water the lawn receives in a given time.

Chapter VII

The Enemies of the Lawn

WEEDS

Weeds constitute one of the gravest problems facing those who wish to create and maintain a beautiful lawn.

If a lawn is thin and covered with weeds, it is logical to suspect one of two reasons — faulty maintenance methods or negligence. The first sensible step to take when trying to control weeds is to discover **why** your lawn has become infested. Whatever the reason — too close a cut, an over-acid soil, a lack of nutritive elements, etc — it is important to apply the appropriate corrective measures.

Furthermore, for weed-control purposes you must always bear in mind the constant struggle between the different plants. If you create conditions favourable to the growth of lawn-grasses, they will tend to occupy all the available space — which makes the task of weed-control correspondingly easier. In contrast, everything that hinders the development of the grass encourages the weeds to grow and spread. Factors such as too much or too little water, faulty mowing, inadequate fertilizing, insects, diseases, the use of unsuitable kinds of grass — all increase the problems caused by weeds.

Trying to control weeds without correcting the basic underlying cause is of no permanent value, and merely involves useless expense. There is no point in trying to eliminate weeds from a lawn where the grass is so feeble that it cannot cover the soil.

Too many gardeners think that to have a beautiful lawn all they need do is get rid of the weeds and then fertilize. Actually, it is not necessary to wait until the weeds are dead before fertilizing. If there is enough grass on the lawn, spread the fertilizer before applying the weed-killer, or do it immediately afterward. Remember, also, to spread enough fertilizer to give the grass a really healthy growth. There are some fertilizers which contain herbicides and these are extremely useful in the battle against weeds. However,

A lawn completely free of weeds is the result of laying high-quality grass and then caring for it properly.

they must be applied early if they are to be really effective. To get the best results, I would also advise you to use a spreader.

Annual weeds

There are certain annual weeds that generally show up in new lawns, but most of them disappear after they have been mown a few times. However, mowing will not succeed in getting rid of certain weeds with leaves and flowers that hug the ground — such as chickweed, black medic, annual veronica and crab-grass.

The logical way to control annual weeds, which have to shed their seeds in order to reproduce themselves, is to stop them from spreading their seeds — either by rooting up or otherwise destroying the plant itself, or by treating it with weed-killer before it can produce its seeds.

The discovery of the selective weed-killer 2, 4-D offered the first effective method of dealing with several broad-leaved weeds such as the dandelion and the plantain without damaging the surrounding grasses.

The copious crop of weeds ruins the look if this lawn and detracts from the general appearance of the property.

Perennial weeds

The most embarrassing lawn weeds are perennial plants such as the dandelion. These plants start growing almost at ground level and produce their seeds very near the surface of the soil. They will remain from one year to the next, despite repeated mowing of the lawn. Other perennial plants such as yarrow, with flower-bearing stems that usually attain a height of a foot (30 cm) or more, can survive several mowings and cling tenaciously to your lawn in the form of low patches of vegetation that do not flower.

Since perennial weeds grow from the same roots year after year, the whole plant must be rooted out of the ground or destroyed in some other way. Several perennial weeds are particularly hard to get rid of because they store

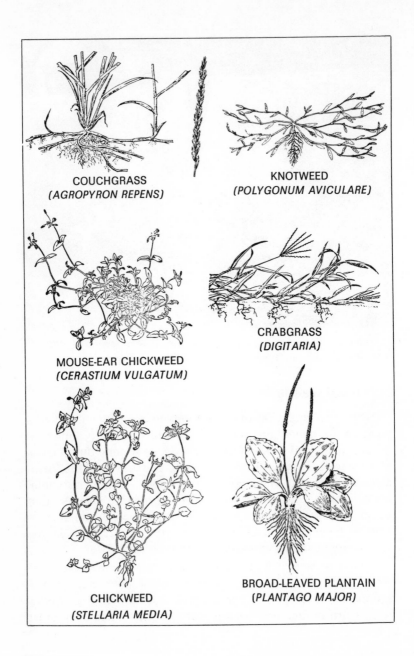

COUCHGRASS
(AGROPYRON REPENS)

KNOTWEED
(POLYGONUM AVICULARE)

MOUSE-EAR CHICKWEED
(CERASTIUM VULGATUM)

CRABGRASS
(DIGITARIA)

CHICKWEED
(STELLARIA MEDIA)

BROAD-LEAVED PLANTAIN
(PLANTAGO MAJOR)

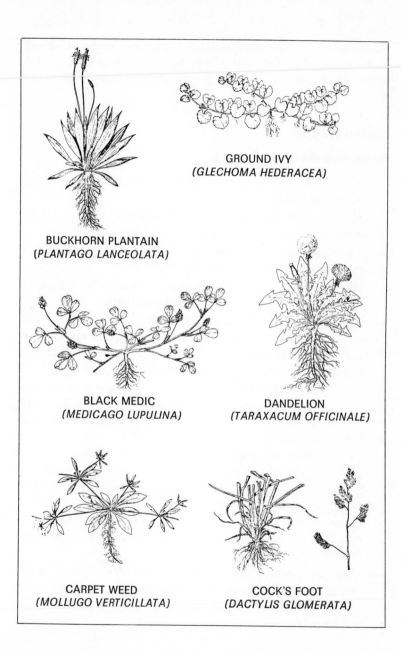

GROUND IVY
(*GLECHOMA HEDERACEA*)

BUCKHORN PLANTAIN
(*PLANTAGO LANCEOLATA*)

BLACK MEDIC
(*MEDICAGO LUPULINA*)

DANDELION
(*TARAXACUM OFFICINALE*)

CARPET WEED
(*MOLLUGO VERTICILLATA*)

COCK'S FOOT
(*DACTYLIS GLOMERATA*)

reserves of nourishment in their roots and these reserves make it possible for new plants to grow, even though the whole of the weed above the ground has been destroyed.

Killing weeds

Preventing the onset of weeds

To prevent the onset of weeds you must adopt the following measures:

— Use a variety of grass or a mixture suitable for local conditions and for the intended use of the lawn.

— Use top-quality grass-seed (purity, guaranteed percentage germination, percentage of weed seeds).

— Water copiously, at well-defined intervals. On the other hand, avoid watering too lightly and too often.

— For a lawn with fairly heavy foot-traffic, a good aeration is recommended. Several types of aerator are available for rent. It is easier to aerate a lawn in spring or at the beginning of the summer when the ground is still moist.

— If the lawn is too thin, the best thing to do is spread a thin layer of compost over the whole of the surface and reseed it. August is the best time for this particular job, but if necessary it can be done early in spring. This method is commonly known as "composting".

— Adjust the height of the cut to suit the variety or varieties of grass in the lawn. Bent grass can be mown very short — as little as 3/16 inch (0.5 cm); bluegrasses need a minimum of 1¼ inches (3 cm), except for 'Merion', which needs only ¾ inch (2 cm); fescue needs a minimum of 1¼ inch (3 cm).

— Mow frequently during the growth-period, but never remove more than one third of the total leaf-surface.

— Keep the fertility of the soil sufficiently high and keep it well-balanced

— Use the weed-killers recommended below and at the proper time.

— in the autum, do your last mowing at a height of 1½ or 2 inches (4 or 5 cm).

Eradicating weeds before laying the lawn

Cultivation: Before sowing seed, it is essential to prepare the ground properly. Break the soil up to a depth of 2 to 4 inches (5 to 10 cm), preferably with the aid of a rotary tiller, and level the surface. If you have the time to spare, turn the top 2 inches (5 cm) of the soil over completely as soon as a good crop of weeds has made its appearance. This method can be repeated throughout the whole season, if neccessary.

Chemical method (sterilizing the soil or the compost):

Methame-sodium (Vapam): 1 quart (1.5 l) of this product will cover 100 sq ft (9.2 m²). The soil should be moist to a depth of 3 inches (7.5 cm) before you apply Vapam. Wait 10 to 14 days, or more, before sowing seed.

Mylone (Dazomet): 1½ lb (600 g will cover 100 sq ft (9.2 m²). This product is a powder. It can be used dissolved in sufficient water to cover the surface to be treated, or it can be used in powder form and dusted over the surface. In either case it should be well mixed into the soil and the surface should be sealed by watering. As before, wait 10 to 14 days, or more, before sowing seed.

With both these products, follow the manufacturer's instructions very carefully.

If your soil is basically unsuitable for seeding purposes, it is preferable to treat it by cultivation and enrich the top 3 to 6 inches (7.5 to 15 cm) with a compost treated chemically or by vaporization.

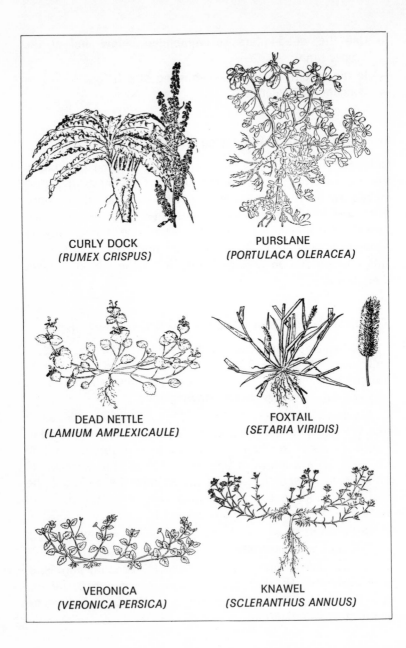

CURLY DOCK
(RUMEX CRISPUS)

PURSLANE
(PORTULACA OLERACEA)

DEAD NETTLE
(LAMIUM AMPLEXICAULE)

FOXTAIL
(SETARIA VIRIDIS)

VERONICA
(VERONICA PERSICA)

KNAWEL
(SCLERANTHUS ANNUUS)

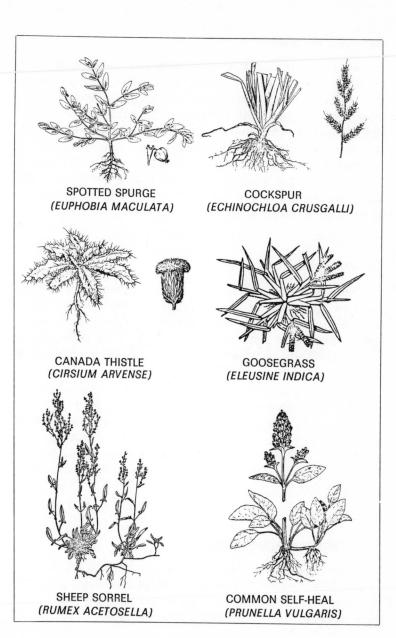

SPOTTED SPURGE
(EUPHOBIA MACULATA)

COCKSPUR
(ECHINOCHLOA CRUSGALLI)

CANADA THISTLE
(CIRSIUM ARVENSE)

GOOSEGRASS
(ELEUSINE INDICA)

SHEEP SORREL
(RUMEX ACETOSELLA)

COMMON SELF-HEAL
(PRUNELLA VULGARIS)

Renewing the lawn

If it becomes necessary to renew your lawn on account of an excessive crop of weeds, follow this method: Mow the lawn, and rake it thoroughly to remove all dead growth. Give it a treatment with paraquat ('Gramoxone') or 'Weed-rite', following the manufacturer's instructions exactly. This treatment will burn off all vegetation. As soon as everything is dead (after a week or ten days), bring in the rotary tiller and turn the soil over to a depth of 2 inches (5 cm). Level the surface with a rake and as soon as the ground is properly prepared, sow the seed.

Growth inhibitors

These products — such as maleic hydrazide ('MH-30', 'Slo-Gro', 'Maintain-3'), or chlorfluorenol ('Maintain CF-125'), or a mixture of the two are recommended for places which are hard to get at with the mower, such as alongside walls or on steep slopes where it is not so important to have a really beautiful stretch of lawn.

Treatments should be carried out in the spring, when the grass is just beginning to grow strongly. To destroy broad-leaved weeds you can use 2,4-D and/or other herbicides designed for the same purpose, together with growth inhibitors. Sometimes you may notice some discoloration after applying growth inhibitors, but this will be only temporary.

Effective use of weed-killers

In view of the many different weed-killers on the market, each with a different percentage content of active ingredient, it is obviously impossible for me to say anything here about how much to use in any one particular case. All I can do

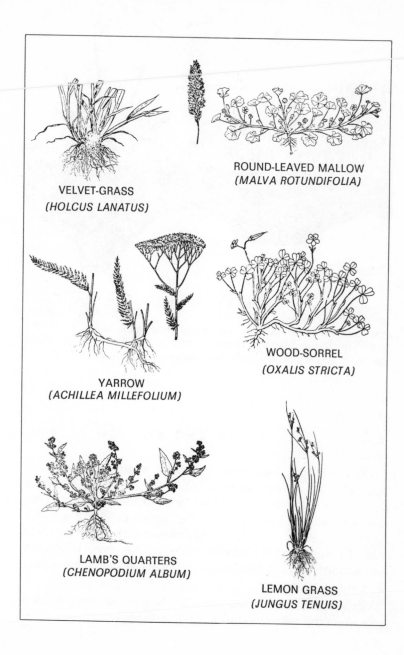

VELVET-GRASS
(HOLCUS LANATUS)

ROUND-LEAVED MALLOW
(MALVA ROTUNDIFOLIA)

YARROW
(ACHILLEA MILLEFOLIUM)

WOOD-SORREL
(OXALIS STRICTA)

LAMB'S QUARTERS
(CHENOPODIUM ALBUM)

LEMON GRASS
(JUNGUS TENUIS)

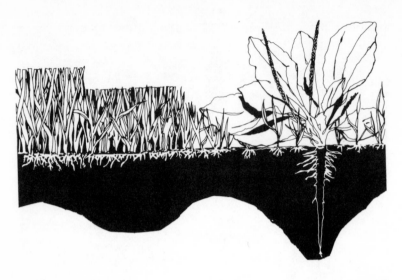

A well-executed mowing, at a suitable height, is a better way of controlling the growth of grass than the use of chemical products. These growth-inhibitors stop the grass from growing — while the weeds (e.g., the plantain shown at the right above) forge ahead vigorously and eventually stifle the lawn-grasses.

is advise you to read the labels and follow the manu-facturer's instructions to the letter.

You will get better results from systemic herbicides such as 2,4-D if you use them when the plants you wish to destroy are still young and at the peak of their growth. Treatments should be carried out in the spring or in the autumn. Autumn treatments have the advantage that they represent less of a danger to the plants bordering the lawn, which are less sensitive to the effects of herbicides at that season than they are in the spring.

If possible, herbicides should be sprayed onto a lawn only when the following three conditions apply:

— **The temperature should be moderate:** too high a temperature may alter the physiological characteristics of plants and therefore alter the effects and specific features of the treatment. There may also be loss of herbicide due to evaporation if the temperature is too high.

— **There should be no wind:** wind may blow away the power, or the vapours it produces, thus reducing the effectiveness of the treatment and also causing damage to neighbouring plants at the same time.

— **There should be no heavy rain forecast:** heavy rain can wash the herbicide away completely, or some of it may be caught up in the run-off and moved physically from the treated area to an area not meant for treatment.

WARNING Lawns are generally surrounded by a great variety of decorative plants, flowers, etc, which can easily be damaged by herbicides. You must therefore take special care when you are using 2,4-D 'Fenoprop', 'Dicamba' or 'Mecoprop'. In addition, newly-sown lawns and bent grasses will themselves be damaged by 2,4-D and 'Fenoprop'.

The sprayer used for weed-killers must only be used for weed-killers, and never for anything else.

Newly-sown lawns

If the ground or the soil was not treated before the seed was sown, you must expect to find weeds growing in your lawn.

A good mowing will often get rid of most annual weeds almost completely. You should not mow too soon after the grass has sprouted. It is better to wait three or four weeks.

Several creeping weeds may survive this initial mowing. In this case, treat them whith 'Mecoprop'.

The year after sowing

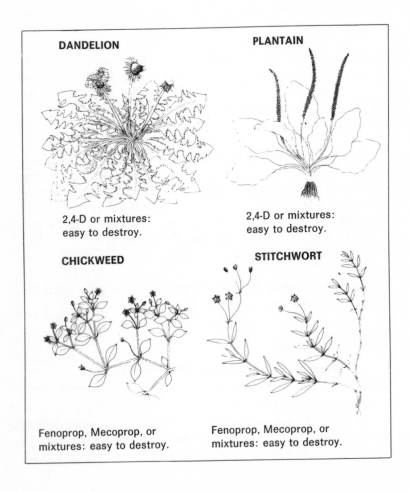

DANDELION

2,4-D or mixtures: easy to destroy.

PLANTAIN

2,4-D or mixtures: easy to destroy.

CHICKWEED

Fenoprop, Mecoprop, or mixtures: easy to destroy.

STITCHWORT

Fenoprop, Mecoprop, or mixtures: easy to destroy.

MOUSE-EAR CHICKWEED

Mecoprop, or mixtures:
easy to destroy.

WOOD-SORREL

Fenoprop, Mecoprop, or
mixtures: easy to destroy.

ROUND-LEAVED MALLOW

Mixtures: hard to destroy,
use repeated treatments.

GROUND IVY

Mixtures: treat while plant
is still young.

WHITE CLOVER

Fenoprop, Mecoprop, or mixtures:
hard to destroy, use repeated treatments.

Mixtures
Several suitable mixtures are available
on the market.

    2,4-D, Mecoprop
    2,4-D, Dicamba
    2,4-D, Mecoprop, Dicamba
    2,4-D, Fenoprop — (SILVEX)
    2,4-D, Fenoprop, Dicamba

2,4-D or mixtures containing 2,4-D should not be
applied to the bent grass family.

CRABGRASS

Pre-emergent treatments
(Before the crabgrass has germinated.)
    Chlorthal — (DACTHAL)
    Siduron — (TUPERSAN)
    Bensulide — (BETASAN)

Post-emergent treatments
(Immediately the crabgrass appears.)
    Disodium arsenate, and other
    organic arsenic compounds

KNOTWEED

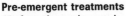

Mixtures, or Dicamba: treat
while plant is still young.

How weed-killers act

In order to kill a weed, the weed-killer must be absorbed by the plant, travel within the plant to the plant's 'nerve-centre' and, finally, have a toxic effect on the plant. Absorption may take place through the leaves or through the stems — as is the case with 2,4-D, 'Mecoprop' and 'Dicamba'; or through the roots, as happens in pre-emergent treatments with 'Betasan' or 'Tupersan'. To get the maximum effect, there must be maximum absorption. This means that the plant must be completely covered by using enough water and a sprayer that is in good working order. Furthermore, the weed-killer must remain on the leaves long enough to let it penetrate into them. Obviously, then, there is no point in carrying out a treatment just before a downpour. Experiments have shown that to obtain satisfactory results you must apply 2,4-D at least 2 or 3 hours before rain, at a temperature of 70 to 75° F (21 to 23° C).

It may perhaps be less obvious that absorptions is very low during dry, hot weather. This is due to the rapid evaporation of water from the liquid sprayed onto the grass, which leaves the herbicide crystallized out the leaves. This has led some experts to recommend that weed-killers be applier at night-time — not merely because the results are better then, but also with a view to avoiding the loss of any of the weed-killer in the wind (which is usually much less strong at night). For night-time applications you should use less water, to reduce trickling of the liquid on the plants which are covered with dew at night.

For absorption through the roots to be successful, the soil must be properly covered by the weed-killer. For pre-emergent control of chickweed, use enough water to ensure that the herbicide will get right down into the soil. The same principle holds good when you are sterilizing the soil with a product such as 'Simazine' or 'Diuron', both of which are used on parking-lots and driveways.

Choosing a weed-killer

The choice of weed-killer depends on what sort of weeds you want to control, and where they are growing. On lawns, mixtures of 2,4-D and 'Mecoprop' or of 2,4-D, 'Mecoprop' and 'Dicamba', give good results in controlling broad-leaved weeds without endangering the blue-grasses or the fescues. You must be very careful when use 2,4-D for it can damage the bent grasses, particularly during very hot weather.

For the edges of driveways and for killing vegetation along walls (especially the walls of buildings), paraquat ('Gramoxone') is excellent. This herbicide burns all vegetation on contact and must therefore be used with great care. However, it has no residual effect, and may therefore be used safely in the renovation of a lawn.

If you want longer-lasting control — for instance, on gravel driveways — use a sterilizing product such as 'Simazine' or 'Diuron'. With these, great care must be taken to ensure that the herbicide is not carried away from its original site by run-off water toward the lawn, shrubs and flowers.

Several herbicides will kill seeds and rhizomes of weeds in soil which you wish to use as a bed for grass-seed or making compost. Products such as allyl alcohol, 'V.P.M.', 'Vorlex' or methyl bromide are excellent for controlling all weed seeds and organisms responsible for diseases in the soil. You must follow the manufacturer's instructions to the letter, for the use of such products is not without danger. It is most important to read the directions for the product you have decided to use very carefully several times before you even think of opening the packet.

Weed-killers and their formulation

The term "formulation" is sometimes used to describe the chemical structure or "formula" of the herbicide, and sometimes to describe the form in which it is put on the market. For example, 2,4-D is marketed either as an amine or as an ether (amines are non-volatile substances, soluble in water).

The term "formulation" is more commonly used in its secondary meaning — i.e., the form in which the herbicide is packaged: as a soluble powder (e.g., 'Dalapon' and 'Amitrole'); as a wettable powder (e.g., 'Simazine' and 'Diuron'); as an emulsifiable liquid (e.g., 2,4-D in the ether form); or as a water-soluble liquid (e.g., 2,4-D in the amine form, and paraquat). Certain forms will not mix directly with other forms. As a general rule, I would not recommend mixing herbicides unless the proposed mixture has already been tested.

How to avoid damage caused by weed killers

Herbicides are generally considered to be less dangerous than fugicides and insecticides. This does not mean to say that they can be handled with less care, for every chemical product can be toxic in high concentrations and in certain conditions. Furthermore, herbicides can cause other serious damage, beside those that might directly affect the operator himself.

The first thing to do when using herbicides is to read the label. I am sorry to say that unfortunately most people only read the label when something has gone wrong and they are trying to find out where they made their mistake. To avoid damaging nearby plants, you should use your sprayer at a fairly low pressure and keep the nozzle down close to the ground. This reduces the risk that the spray might be carried away by puffs of wind. Obviously, you should **not** spray herbicides in a high wind, and you should also keep well clear of plants that might be damaged, such as flowers and shrubs. Nor should you spray certain grasses during very hot weather — particularly bent grasses and fescues which might very well be completely ruined. Also avoid spraying a new lawn at least until it has been mown two or three times.

When you get rid of the empty packets, remember that no packet is ever **completely** empty. Never use packets which contained herbicides, or any other form of pesticide, as containers for something else. Glass containers should be broken and buried somewhere where they cannot contaminate the water. Cardboard or other combustible containers should be burnt — except those which contained 2,4-D or similar products since these can give out fumes which are toxic to certain plants.

Never pour what is left in the box or other container down the sink or into the toilet. Burying the residue is far less risky. Make the containers unusable by driving holes through them or squashing them flat, then bury them somewhere where there is little risk of the residue being leached out by water and making its way towards plants which could be damaged by it.

Storing weed-killers

You should not store weed-killers near fertilizers, fungicides or other chemical products. It is also advisable to keep herbicides in their original packets or containers. Store them so that there is little risk of their overturning, thus contaminating other products. If at all possible, it is better to store them somewhere where they will not run the risk of being frozen. Certain formulations tend to separate out or crystallize after being frozen.

What does the future hold?

We know that today's herbicides for lawns do not affect the grass if they are used correctly. However, our knowledge of their long-term effects is incomplete. It is possible that the same herbicide applied year after year tends to accumulate in the soil and may reduce the growth of the grass it is meant to be protecting. Do some herbicides tend to weaken the grass — i.e., do they make it more vulnerable to diseases and certain adverse conditions such as dryness? Far more research is necessary before we can answer questions like that.

Other research projects have been directed to the problem of determining the best time to apply herbicides. For example, we are fairly certain that excellent control can be obtained by applying them in the autumn. However, we cannot yet precisely determine the perfect time or the exact effect certain climatic conditions have on these chemical products. We would also like to know what changes in weed populations are brought about by a continuing use of herbicides on our lawns. If we constantly destroy the weeds that are easy enough to kill, then we are certainly inviting invasion by more resistant species such as yarrow, mallow and couchgrass. The control of perennial lawn weeds such as couchgrass has hardly been researched at all. This is, admittedly, a much more difficult problem, since we are attempting to kill one type of grass in the midst of other grasses. However, I can predict that we shall be able to do this at some time in the future.

How to exercise better control over weeds

Here are some suggestions which will enable you to exercise better control over the weeds in your lawn:

First and most important, always follow the manufacturer's instructions exactly whenever you use a herbicide. I cannot stress this point too strongly. It is true that most of the failures experienced in the use of these chemical products are due to faulty application, either in the method of application, the quantity applied or the time of application.

I suggest that you carry out herbicide treatments in May or September. I personally prefer autumn applications — for I can be certain then that dandelions will be suppressed for the following year. If you wait till spring, you will sometimes get a whole series of rainy days that hold the treatment up until the dandelions are actually in flower. Control is more effective if herbicide is applied during reasonably hot weather. This does not mean to say that you should wait until the temperature is 80° F (26.7° C) — merely that you will get better results if it is warm enough to let the herbicide do its work quickly. If you have never used weed-killers before, let me suggest that you carry out the job at night-time, for the reasons noted earlier.

One final suggestion — try to keep notes on your activities with herbicides. In these notes you should record the exact period of growth at the time you applied the herbicides — i.e., how long it was since the lawn had last been mown. The type of application should also be entered — e.g., spray, granules, etc. If you keep notes like this for several years, I am quite sure that they will help you solve many of your weed-control problems and enable you to achieve better results.

Moss

Moss is a problem only on lawns where conditions are so bad that the grass is retarded in its growth or lacking in vigour. The presence of moss in a lawn does not necessarily mean that the soil is acid.

Poor fertility, too much shade and faulty drainage are factors which encourage the growth of moss, and to a certain extent hinder that of grass. Whenever possible, these conditions should be corrected. Moss-infested areas should be dug up, then resown with suitable grass-seed after improvement of the soil and elimination of excess shade have created conditions more favourable to the growing of grass. In lightly-infested areas, moss can be removed with a steel rake.

Controlling weeds with weed-killers

PLANT	TYPE	SUGGESTED APPLICATION TIME	SUGGESTED HERBICIDE	REMARKS
Dicotyledonous Weeds				
Broad-leaved weeds:				
Dandelion, plantain, sorrel, mustard	P	Spring or autumn	2,4-Damine 80	Apply before the dandelion buds are formed
Broad-leaved weeds that are difficult to kill:				
Wood-sorrel, yarrow, dead nettle, cinquefoil	A or P	Spring or autumn	Killex Dicamba	
Chickweeds:				
Common chickweed, mouse ear chickweed, carpet weed	P P A	April-May April-May June-july	Dicamba	Treatment of chickweed must be carried out before grass-seed is sown
Clovers:				
White, red, hop	B P	Spring or autumn	Dicamba	

Knotweed	A	May-June	Dicamba	Best treated while the plant is young
Veronica	A P	Spring Autumn	Dicamba	
Spurge	A	June-July	Dacthal (granular 2.5%)	Best treated while the plant is young

Monocotyle-donous Weeds

Crabgrasses:

Purple, smooth	A	Pre-emergence: May	Dacthal (granular 2.5%)	
Goosegrass	A	April	Dacthal	
Annual bluegrass	A	Pre-emergence: autumn	Dacthal	

A: Annual   B: Biennial   P: Perennial

INSECT PESTS

Insects and other pests

Insects are insidious invaders of the lawn, where their presence only becomes evident after extensive damage has already been done. Certain larvae and other similar insects, such as the chinch bug, feed on the grass leaves.

It is a good idea to examine the lawn every time you mow it. If you find brown spots then prepare for trouble! Some insect pests can be detected by spreading the grass-plants apart so that you can inspect the base of the plants,

Insects harmful to grass

Weevil

Centipede

Lawn-moth (adult)

Millipede

Webworm (lawn-moth larva)

Whiteworm

Snail

Leaf-hopper

Cricket

Japanese beetle

(Photos: United States Department of Agriculture)

or by digging furrows in the soil. If you cannot find any insects, I suggest cutting some specimen cores of turf and having them examined by an agronomist or a lawn expert. The problem might be some form of lawn disease.

Ants

Occasionally you may find an ant's nest in your lawn — especially in sandy soils. These nests can cause considerable damage to the lawn. Chlordane is a most effective insecticide for ants. It is available in emulsion, wettable powder, dry powder or granular form.

The emulsion must be used strictly in accordance with the manufacturer's instructions. Mix 5 ounces (142 g) of 40% chlordane powder in 2 gallons (9 l) of water. This will make enough solution to spray 1000 sq ft (92 m^2) of surface area. Water the lawn afterward, to help the solution penetrate into the soil.

Alternatively, spread ½ lb (227 g) of 5% chlordane powder over the same area. Then water the lawn to dissolve the insecticide into it.

For treating individual ants' nests, use ⅛ teaspoonful of wettable 40% chlordane powder, then water. The same results are obtained by using 1 teaspoonful of 5% graunlar chlordane for each ants' nest.

Chinch bugs

These bugs kill the grass by sucking the leaves and the crowns of the grass-plants. They do not feed on the roots. Their attacks result in the appearance of dead areas in the lawn, and these areas grow larger and larger as the season progresses. Note that these insects attack only the grasses in the lawn. They will not touch broad-leaved weeds at all.

Adult chinch bugs are ⅕ inch (1 cm) in length and have a white band on their wings. The immature insects are

Life-cycle of the chinch bug
A Eggs B to F The five stages of immaturity G Winged adult
(Photos: United States Department of Agriculture)

brick-red in colour in the earliest stage: the older ones are black, with a white band behind their wings. The adult insects pass the winter in some suitably sheltered spot: as soon as the temperature reaches 70° F (21.1° C) or more, they fly out onto grassed surfaces, to lay their eggs. There are two broods per year. Infestation reaches its peak between the middle and the end of the summer.

You will not find these insects in the patches of dead grass they have caused, but in the living grass nearby.

Before treating the lawn with an insecticide, water it copiously. Carbaryl ('Sevin') and 'Diazinon' are effective against the chinch bug. 'Sevin', in the form of a wettable 50% powder, should be used in the proportions of 2 lb (900 g) per 5000 sq ft (460 m^2) of lawn surface. On small areas, use 4 teaspoons in 1 gallon of water.

Another method of treatment is to use a 25% emulsion of 'Diazinon' in the proportions of 1½ quarts (1 l) per 5000 sq ft (460 m^2) of lawn, or ¼ oz of fluid (7.5 g) in 1 gallon (4.5 l) of water. For large areas, spray 125 gallons (562 l) of 'Sevin' or 'Diazinon' per 500 sq ft (460 m^2) of lawn.

If there are many insects, the lawn should be treated in June and then again in July and August, to deal with the second brood — which may well require two applications.

Areas affected by chinch bugs should be dug up, treated with insecticide, and then resceded.

Whiteworms

Whiteworms or white larvae are the larvae of the common June bug. These June bugs lay their eggs in the turf or among weeds.

After hatching, the larvae begin feeding on the lawngrasses and other plant roots just beneath the surface of the soil. The larvae are particularly harmful during the year following the laying of the eggs. The lawn suffers serious damage when from 2 to 5 larvae are present per square foot (929 cm^2).

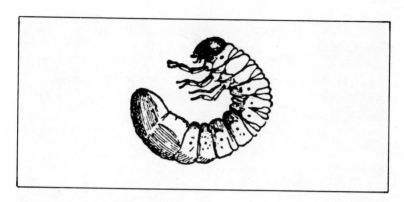

Larva of the common June bug

Even though the presence of June bugs may be noticed every year, normally the really serious infestations seem to come in cycles of three years.

Chlordane is very effective against the larvae of the June bug. The best time to apply this insecticide is in May or June of the year in which the June bug infestation is really serious, or early the following year. There is also a fertilizer, of 12-4-8 formulation, which contains a larvicide, an insecticide and 1% of chlordane.

Chlordane formulations and dosages:

5% granular: 4 to 5 lb (1.8 to 2.2 kg) per 1000 sq ft (92 m²)

40% emulsifiable: 8 fluid ounces (25 cm³) per 1000 sq ft (92 m²).

On small areas, spread the granular form by hand; for larger areas, use a spreader.

Wettable powder gives good results, provided that it is spread in accordance with the manufacturer's instructions. The required amount of emulsion or wettable powder should be added to 3 gallons (13.5 l) of water for each 1000 sq ft

The greedy larvae of the common June bug feed on the roots of lawn-grasses.

(92 m²) of surface area, then sprayed over the lawn or sprinkled evenly with a watering-can. Then give the lawn a good watering, to get the insecticide down into the soil.

If you mix chlordane with fertilizer or insecticides, make sure you use the right amount of insecticide to ensure effective control of the larvae.

Earthworms are often a nuisance in bent grass lawns which are cut very short. The little lumps of earth they leave on the lawn give it an untidy appearance, although it should be emphasized that they do not actually damage it. To get rid of earthworms, use chlordane in double the quantities recommended for the treatment of whiteworms.

Moles can be destroyed by poison, traps or gassing. The traps should be set so as to catch them when they leave their tunnel. Incidentally, it is known that moles feed mainly on earthworms and insects so if you control these latter pests successfully you should not have any trouble with moles.

Moles can be gassed with the exhaust fumes from a car or a garden tractor. Fix one end of your garden hose to the exhaust pipe and push the other end down the mole's tunnel. Then let the motor run for at least 20 minutes. After the moles are dead the open end of the tunnel can be filled in neatly.

Typical appearance of a lawn attacked by larvae of the common June bug. Note the large whitish area: this is a sure sign of the depredations of these insects.

GRASS DISEASES

Grass diseases can destroy a lawn in a very short time. The best way of preventing them is to use proper management practices — i.e., to give your grass the appropriate attention and not place your trust solely in the use of fungicides.

A beautiful lawn of rich green grass, with each blade trimmed to carpet height, is a fine aesthetic ideal — but it is also a biological nightmare. The plain fact is that a lawn must often undergo many different conditions e.g., full sunlight, partial shade, full shade, dry slopes or low, damp areas. One particular species of lawn-grass well-suited to full sunlight may find it hard to survive in the shade, and vice versa.

As a perennial crop, lawn-grass produces plenty of clippings and root-debris within the soil, as well as leaving dead plants on the surface of the soil. A constant recycling takes place — nutritive elements turning into organic matter, and the organic matter breaking down again into elements — if all goes according to plan. However, only too often the grass clippings are allowed to accumulate with the other plant debris and the lawn becomes covered with culm. In many cases, this culm is so thick that the soil on a slope is never moist, even after a heavy rainfall or a copious watering. The culm and the clippings form a perfect shelter for a whole host of pathogenic organisms. Some of these microorganisms use the lawn merely as a shelter, but for others it becomes a source of nourishment and they may remain from one to ten years. All they need is a suitable environment, and they soon move from the dead clippings to the live grass.

Diseases are a constant hazard for lawn grasses. It cannot be said with any truth that there is a single moment in the whole year in which you may relax your guard against diseases. In winter-time, beneath the blanket of snow, snow-mould may be busily at work attacking the blades of grass, while in the summer-time rust and other fungii can transform a beautiful living green carpet into a tattered remnant — a mere shadow of what it was before.

The shorter the grass is cut, the greater the stress placed on the organism of the plants. The root-system is smaller and weaker if the grass is short, the damage caused by dryness is more serious and the grass is affected more by foot-traffic.

For a beautiful carpet of greenery each grass-plant must be similar to its fellows. This means that if a micro-organism can attack one leaf of grass, then all the others are in danger. The conditions are ripe for an epidemic.

Different species of grasses growing together mean resistance to diseases. Uniformity of species and varieties inevitably results in epidemics of diseases and insects. Conversely, the more diverse the population of grassplants in a lawn, the lower the threat from hostile organisms such as microscopic fungii.

For many years, breeders have been seeking the perfect lawn-grass — the grass that will resist all diseases and all insects and will also produce a lawn as smooth as a carpet. Too often, all they succeed in doing is merely changing the nature of the problem — replacing one particular disease or insect by another.

Objectives have become more realistic. What we are looking for today is new varieties of lawn-grass which can live together for long periods. If a micro-organism attacks one of the strains, the others are resistant, no epidemic results and the disease has little effect.

With the new varieties of lawn-grass now available and with proper care, it is quite possible to develop and maintain a beautiful lawn.

Here are some tips to help you keep your grass healthy: Cut the grass no shorter than 2 inches (5 cm) or more, in order to keep the root-system strong. Put off fertilizing with nitrogen-rich fertilizers until the beginning of the summer, when the growth-surge of the spring is over. Do not cut your lawn often — be satisfied with a little lighter shade of green. Sow new varieties of grass-seed mixture. Remove all clippings during periods of rapid growth. Remove culm and aerate the lawn.

Anyone can have a lovely-looking lawn during the first year of its growth — indeed, during the first three years. But what will a lawn look like after or ten years? Will it still be beautiful?

To keep it beautiful, you should rely more on proper lawn maintenance than on a host of so-called "remedies".

The principal grass diseases

Brown spot

This disease is sometimes called "summer burn", since it is a problem that arises only when the weather is hot and humid. It is caused by a microscopic fungus and appears in circular patches which are faded and brown. The blades of grass collapse, producing the effect of a depression or "pocket" in the lawn. The most obvious characteristic makes its appearance early in the morning when greyish "smoke circles" from around the edges of the burnt patches. These circles disappear as the grass dries out.

All lawn grasses are affected by brown spot, though only the finest, such as the bent grasses, are seriously hit. The bluegrasses and the fescues resist reasonably well, though they may need protection during humid spells. Grass fungicides give adequate protection, provided they are used at the first sign of the disease.

Damages caused by insects and diseases in a lawn Upper left: Irregular patches, as shown, and a general drying-up or staining of the lawn are indications that the lawn is being attacked by insects in the soil. Lower left: Lawn-moths cause brownish patches, while army worms leave their traces in the lawn. Attacks by bugs may turn the grass either white or brown. Upper right: If your lawn turns brown or greyish, even though you have watered and fertilized it properly, and there is no damage from insects, then it has been attacked by some disease. Lower right: Here are some of the characteristic traces to be seen on the blades of lawn-grasses: A. Leaf-fungus B. Rust fungus C. Leaf-rot D. Powdery mildew.

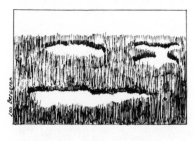

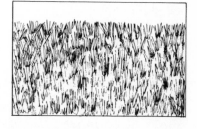

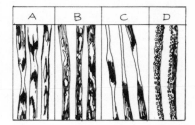

Helminthospore blight

This is essentially a disease of cool, humid weather. It strikes mainly in May and June and sometimes in September. The microscopic fungus attacks the leaves of the grass-plant, forming spots which take on a straw-yellow colour in the centre as they grow. In humid conditions, these spots run together and the whole leaf is discoloured. The fungus creeps down toward the base of the stem, damaging the crown of the plant and the roots.

Control measures include mowing — which must not be closer than 1 inch (2.5 cm) — and the removal of all grass clippings, since humid mulch of that sort is a perfect breeding-ground for the fungus. If you detected the presence of this disease in your lawn the previous year, you should also apply fungicides every two weeks throughout May and June. If you wait until the disease shows itself before spraying with fungicide, the treatment will not be of much value, for by that time the fungus will have penetrated deeply into the grass-plants and the fungicide will not be able to get at it properly.

Powdery mildew

Powdery mildew occurs chiefly on lawns lying in the shade, or which are in the shade during at least part of the day, and which have an inadequate air circulation over them. If this disease is widespread, particularly in the case of 'Merion' bluegrass which grows in shaded locations, it may also attack the other grasses in the lawn. It is recognizable by a greyish-white growth on the leaves. It is difficult to get rid of powdery mildew completely, but it can be kept under control by spraying with fungicides such as 'Actidione' and 'Karathane'.

Snow-mould

Snow-mould is often encountered on lawns in northerly areas. The fungus becomes active at temperatures close to freezing-point, while the soil is very damp (either from the melting of the snow or from rain). The mould normally becomes visible when the snow melts, it looks like a thick spider's web of mycelium and covers patches of grass varying in diameter from a few inches to several feet.

Apply the appropriate fungicide late in the autumn, before the winter blanket of snow is on the ground. To speed the healing process, use a stiff broom to break up the mycelium web on those portions of the lawn not treated with the fungicide.

The mycelium of the snow-mould fungus appears in the form of a spider's web when the snow melts.

Fungii

Fungii are a nuisance at times on some lawns. Their presence may be due to the rotting of the roots of nearby trees or of other organic matter in the soil. The only effective way of getting rid of them is to dig out the rotting roots or other matter on which they are growing.

Fungii may also be produced by a microscopic organism, Marasmius oreades, which causes the disease known as "fairy ring". The symptom of this is a semi-circle of strongly-growing grass which is deep green at the beginning of the summer. Then in the autumn, or during humid weather, the fungus makes its appearance along the inner rim of this semi-circle. The grass is generally weakened, and may even die in badly-affected places. The microscopic fungus forms thick layers of mycelium in the soil, draining it of nitrogen and water.

You can get rid of this disease by soaking the soil with fungicides containing cadmium, with an added humidifying agent. To ensure satisfactory penetration, use a garden fork to make holes in the ground 4 inches (10 cm) deep and 2 inches (5 cm) apart. After treatment, water the area thoroughly.

NOTE: Use the quantities recommended opposite to cover 1000 sq ft (92 m²). Some of the quantities will not correspond exactly with the manufacturer's recommendations. However, they are effective for our own climatic conditions here in Canada.

Fairy circles, caused by the presence of a microscopic fungus.

Fungicides recommended for controlling ordinary grass diseases

Fungicide	Brown Spot	Helmin-thospore Blight	Powdery Mildew	Snow-mould
Actidione-Thiram	4 oz	4 oz	2 oz	—
Daconil 75% WP	4 oz	4 oz	—	9 oz
Dyrene 50% WP	4 oz	4 oz	—	—
Maneb 80% WP	3 oz	3 oz	—	—
Polyram C	3 oz	3 oz	—	—
Tersan 1991	2 oz	—	2 oz	—
Tersan SP	—	—	—	6 oz

Damages caused by the winter

"Winter kill" may show up on lawns which have been subjected to low temperatures with an insufficient covering of snow, or which have been exposed to cold coupled with parching winds. Constant alternation of low and high temperatures also causes damage. Unsuitable species of lawn-grass are particularly affected by winter conditions. If leaves are left on the surface of the lawn, the grass may be stifled — just as low-lying areas of the lawn may be killed if they are stifled by standing water or ice in the hollows.

One of the most common forms of damage is that caused by foot-traffic on a frozen lawn. Considerable havoc may also be caused by leaving a sheet of ice such as a skating rink — on the surface of the lawn for a lengthy period, especially if the underlying soil had not frozen before the ice formed on top of it.

Insufficient drainage may ruin parts of a lawn by allowing water to stand on the surface, or because the soil has been water-logged for long periods with the result that the root-system of the grass has been stifled. If it is impossible to prevent water from collecting in pools, it might be preferable to replace the bluegrass and fescue by bent grass, which can tolerate excessive water.

Ravages caused by salt during the winter

The use of salt during the winter often causes damage to lawns, but it is an easy and effective way of ridding the streets and driveways of snow and ice.

Canadian researchers have studied the effect of salt on various species of lawn grass. The results they obtained show that sensitivity to salt varies considerably from one species to another. One series of experiments led to the conclusion that house-owners could ward off much of the damage by giving their lawns a really deep soaking in spring, to wash out the salt deposited on them throughout the winter.

Results of scientific tests

During some experiments carried out under green-house conditions, 14 separate cultures of grass, representing seven different lawn species, were watered twice a week with solutions of road-salt — first with a 2% solution, then with a 4% solution. All the cultures proved reasonably capable of withstanding the weaker of the two solutions, but they showed clear differences in their reactions to the 4% solution. The most sensitive were common bent grass, which is often planted in damp ground, and red fescue, a species particularly suitable for planting in the shade and in sandy soils with little fertility. By contrast, tall fescue, a tough, clumpy plant endowed with a network of vigorous fibrous roots, proved extremely tolerant. 'Norlea' perennial rye-grass, currently used as a temporary cover while the permanent lawn-grasses are being installed, was the most tolerant of the 14 cultures uder test.

Kentucky bluegrass, the main lawn-grass grown in Canada, proved superior to both bent grass and red fescue, but inferior to tall fescue and to 'Norlea'.

After the salt treatments, all the cultures were rinsed by immersion in water and were then allowed a period of recuperation.

At the end of 35 days, al the salt-resistant grasses had recovered their usual vigour and their blade-growth equalled that of grasses which had not been treated. This recovery suggests that the harmful effects of salt on lawns can be lessened by soaking the lawn thoroughly in the spring.

Chapter VIII

Tools and Equipment

THE LAWN-MOWER

When it comes to maintaining a lawn, the most important piece of equipment is without doubt the lawn-mower. In fact, this is the very first garden tool that you should buy. The lawn-mower goes into action just a few weeks after the lawn has been laid — it is probably the first work you do in your new garden. Only too often, the first lawn-mower soon proves itself quite inadequate and most gardeners have to start looking for another one.

It is true that almost every mower on the market will in fact cut grass, but there is no one mower that can satisfy all the needs and peculiarities of a thousand different lawns. Before you buy **your** mower, you should know which type is best suited to **your** lawn.

Choosing a lawn-mower

The different types of mower

Reel-type mower — hand operated
Reel-type mower — power driven
Rotary mower — power driven (gasoline or electric)
Rotary mower — power, with seat
Tractor with accessories for mowing

The hand mower is suitable for small lawns of no great area. The reel mower, shown here, gives a very precise cut.

The rotary gas-driven motor mower is the most popular type of mower — especially the model shown here, equipped with a bag to collect the grass-clippings.

If you have decided to buy a power mower, you will probably be completely bewildered — as so many people are — by the great differences in price. One shop may offer a power mower for $125, while in the next store the price for a mower of the same capacity is $175. The two machines may **look** almost identical, yet there is almost certainly an important difference between them — and that is service. One of the things you must always bear in mind when buying a mower — whether it is your first or merely a replacement —it what sort of service can you expect from the vendor or from the maker, and here, "service" includes repairs, adjustment and replacements.

Hand-operated mowers are still the best answer in many cases, although for some time now they have been rather relegated to the background. Even though these mowers have to be pushed by hand and their use therefore demands a certain amount of physical effort, there are still many places where you cannot use a power mower. First of all, it would actually be quite difficult to manoeuvre a power

The electric rotary mower is very economical in use. It combines the advantages of the electric motor with the good qualities of the rotary mower, which is the ideal equipment for cutting long grass.

mower on a very small lawn. Again, there are often places — even on large lawns — which have to be cut with a hand-mower because it would be difficult, if not impossible, to use any other type of equipment — around trees and bushes, for example.

Today's hand-mowers are better made and easier to push than those of twenty years ago. However, you should make sure that the blades are made of tempered steel so that they will stay sharp and stand up to prolonged use.

Hand-mowers are available in widths from 12 to 19 inches (30 to 48 cm), but the most popular widths are 14 or 16 inches (35 to 40cm).

Buy a mower with big wheels — not only are they easier to push, but they cause less damage side-slipping on the lawn. Furthermore, if the blades of the reel are blunt, or the stationary blade is out of adjustment, the mower will be hard to push.

Power reel-type mowers are very similar to hand-operated reel mowers, except that they are bigger and are operated by a gasoline or electric motor.

The folding handle of this rotary mower makes it easy to handle and to transport.

Since the motor drives the cutting reel and the wheels, there is no need to push these mowers. Although ten power rotary mowers are sold for every power reel-type mower, it must be stressed that only a reel-type mower can give you a lawn that really looks like a lovely carpet. On a lawn which is reasonably level, without hillocks or depressions, a reel-type mower will give better results. On the other hand, this type of mower costs more and will not cut long grass or tall weeds. Also, it is necessary to mow the lawn more often and wait until the grass is standing properly upright.

Power reel mowers are available in widths from 16 to 21 inches (40 to 53 cm), and the reels have either five or six blades. Curiously enough, the more blades there are on the reel, the more often the lawn must be mowed. However, if the reel has too few blades then the grass will have a 'wavy' look to it if it was allowed to get a little too long

Several models of rotary mower are equipped with an electric starting system.

before cutting. Sharpening the blades of the reel and the stationary blade is a job for a specialist.

Reel-type mowers can cut grass very short — down to a fraction of an inch. Generally speaking, they slice off the ends of the blades of grass. The grass is cut between the stationary blade and the revolving blades of the reel. In short, these mowers cut the blades of grass in much the same way as a pair of scissors would. This is why people with top-quality lawns prefer them. Furthermore, in most cases the reel-type mower is more of a precision instrument, and will last longer.

Power rotary mowers are not very expensive, either to buy or to maintain. They chop the blades of grass rather than actually cutting them, and they do a good job with long grass and tall weeds. They will cut quite close to obstacles and are easy to manoeuvre. The blade can be sharpened easily enough by the owner. Some of these mowers are self-propelling.

The power of the motor is proportional to the width of the cut, which is generally between 16 and 22 inches (40 and

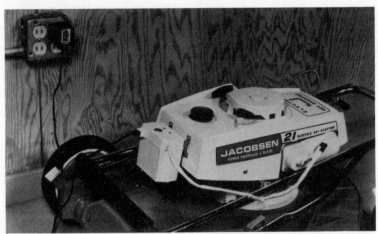

The electric starting system on this rotary mower can be quickly recharged by plugging it into a 110-volt source of supply.

Oiling the wheels and other moving parts of a mower keeps it functioning well and prolongs its life.

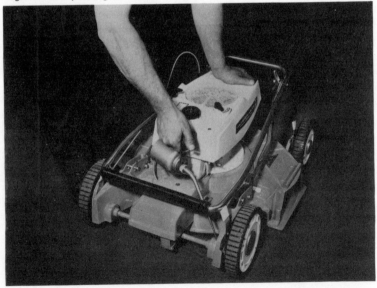

The rotary mower that works on a cushion of air is a fairly heavy piece of equipment. However, it has many advantages for those who want to give their lawns a really first-class cut.

56 cm). Gasoline-driven motors are usually 3 or 4 HP, while electric motors are 1 or 1½ HP. Rotary mowers can be used on very rough ground and on neglected areas which are not often mown.

The rotary mower has its drawbacks — the most important of which is that it can be a dangerous machine, both for the user and for those in the immediate vicinity. With a blade revolving at high speed, the danger of objects being shot out like bullets is always present. It is not entirely safe when you are mowing very rough ground or sloping terraces. It has a tendency to tear off the ends of the blades of grass, rather than cutting them clean, and in certain cases is can actually tear out young grass-plants if the blade is blunt — which leaves a brownish tinge on the lawn. However, if the blade is kept properly sharp, it can produce quite an acceptable lawn.

The motorized reel mower cuts the grass quickly, and gives your lawn a well-groomed appearance. Note the box for clippings on this model. This stops a build-up of clippings on the surface of the lawn.

The least costly rotary mowers have a 2-stroke motor that runs on a mixture of gasoline and oil — which is somewhat of a nuisance for the user. However, a 2-stroke motor works better than a 4-stroke motor on slopes and embankments. It should also be realized that a rotary mower with a self-starter is very heavy.

Power rotary mowers are of two types: those which have to be pushed and those which are self-propelling.

There are certain rotary mowers which have no wheels and move on a cushion of air. They have several advantages — one of which is that there is no need to push them, they can be pulled along very easily. They do an excellent job on slopes and little hills and other areas which are difficult to mow, as long as the user is careful not to lose his footing. However, they have a couple of disadvantages in that they are expensive and they are somewhat heavy to move about when not in use.

The maintenance of a power rotary mower is not very expensive. But just as in the case of the reel-type mower the motor must be kept in good working order — although when the blade needs sharpening, the owner can do it himself with a file.

Electric mowers are being used in ever-increasing numbers, because they are so easy to operate. There are many different models on the market, offering a wide range of characteristics to suit all types of lawn.

Here are a few points to consider if you are thinking of buying an electric motor. The practical side is usually the main attraction for most people because the machine starts so easily — all you need do is plug in to an electrical outlet and switch it on. As to performance, there is no doubt that an electric mower gives a more even and a more easily controlled cut. Running costs should not exceed more than 4 cents' worth of electricity per hour, if the machine is in good order.

This motorized reel mower has a detachable handle, which makes it easy to store.

A mower with a seat lets you cut large lawns with a minimum of time and effort. A model such as the one shown here can cut a quarter-acre lawn in less than 15 minutes.

The are two main types of electric mower: single-bladed and twin-bladed. The single-blade model is about 18 inches (46 cm) in diameter and is meant for large open lawns with few trees, bushes, slopes, or terraces. This model is particularly suitable for lawns where the grass grows very quickly. The twin-bladed model is excellent for smaller lawns with trees, bushes, slopes and hillocks dotted about them. The machine is compact, light and easy to handle. Its short wheel-base allows it to glide smoothly over rough ground without tearing out patches of grass. It handles very easily around trees, bushes and flowerbeds.

Manufacturers of electric mowers also put out models with other characteristics that make them even more practical and give even better results. For example, if you want a really even cut I can recommend an electric mower fitted with a suction hood. Basically, this is a miniature wind-tunnel which draws the blades of grass upright while the mower is cutting them, giving a very even cut. In addition, this type of machine really compresses the grass clippings into the collecting-bag, which allows you to work for a longer period without having to empty the bag.

Two-speed electric mowers are becoming more and more popular, since they offer greater flexibility. At the beginning of the spring and late in the autumn, the lawn is often thick and damp. To get a uniform cut in these conditions, set the wheels in the 'upper' position and use the 3000-rpm motor-speed. On the other hand, the wheels should be in the 'lower' position in mid-summer and the motor speed should be 2800-rpm.

Several electric mowers allow adjustment of the height of the cut. On some older models the necessary adjustment may have to be made with a tool — e.g. a monkey wrench. Many models now offer "finger-tip adjustment", which enables the user to raise or lower the height of the cut quickly, without the use of any tool.

A reversible handle is another feature of electric mowers which wins more and more adherents every year. Thus, when using an electric mower fitted with this type of handle, all you need do when you come to a narrow corner or to the end of a row is switch the handle over to the other side and carry on in the opposite direction. In addition, this handle will fold flat, which makes the mower much easier to store.

The collecting-bag is optional on some models and standard equipment on others. The grass clippings are blown into the bag, ready for dumping.

There is one very important point you must remember — the guarantee on whatever model you finally decide to buy. A two-year guarantee is usual in the industry. Some manufacturers also offer a free inspection service before the start of the season. This means that your mower will always be in tip-top condition and you can be sure that if anything does happen to need attention you will be able to get it put right quickly at the manufacturer's service centre.

Mowers with a seat suit large properties, since they are wide machines and cut large grassed areas very rapidly. However, they can never replace the small hand-mower

Small garden tractors, with their numerous accessories which can be rapidly attached, make the maintenance of large lawns much easier. Gear-driven rotary mowers 34, 42, or even 48 inches in diameter (86, 105, or 120 cm) can be attached to them, and these make short work of cutting the grasss near flowerbeds, trees, and bushes — thus saving you a lot of manual labour and giving you more time to relax.

which can be pushed into odd corners to deal with weeds, nor can they work too close to thickets or other obstacles. they are safer than mowers that must be pushed, since the operator sits up on top of the mower, well out of the way of any flying objects.

Various models are available, from 5 HP, with a 28-inch (71 cm) cut, to 8 or 10 HP, with a cut of 36 to 42 inches (91.5 to 120 cm).

Seated models have certain disadvantages. For example, if the motor is not powerful enough the mower will be unable to get up slopes. Also, if they are badly designed, they can overturn on slopes and sharp corners. Some models can turn over backward if you engage the clutch with

Here is a long-awaited refinement in gardening equipment — the electric mini-tractor. This new tractor for lawns and gardens is the 'Elec-Trak'. It works off six electric batteries, which can be recharged from any ordinary 110-volt domestic source of supply. Some 40 tools or accessories may be hitched onto it — among them a rotary mower, which can be used in all weathers. This new piece of equipment also represents another step forward in the fight against pollution.

the motor running at full speed. A safety clutch is better than an automatic one, since it has to be held in all the time to keep the motor running. Thus, if the operator falls off his seat, or the mower starts skidding, as soon as he takes his foot off the clutch the machine will come to a stop.

Two words of advice about seated mowers. Never carry a passenger on the mower. Read your insurance policy very carefully before you allow children to use the machine.

A mini-tractor with power take-off is the obvious choice if your lawn is large enough to justify a seated mower and if you have sufficient outhouse space to store a tractor.

These little tractors tend to squash the grass down more than the other types of mower, particularly when the lawn is damp. Mini-tractors are multipurpose machines. Their motors range from 6 HP to 14 HP, and there is a good selection of optional accessories. The 9 HP model is the most popular one, but it is not powerful enough for certain jobs, such as snow-clearing.

Points to watch when choosing a mower

— Adjustable handles which are comfortable for both tall and short users.

— Controls which are easy to get at in the event of an emergency.

— Not too much plastic, which can warp, crack or break.

— Handles which can be folded back for easy storage.

— Grass discharged to one side. Machines with forward or backward discharge are dangerous to the user

— Wheels large enough to make movement over rough ground relatively easy

— Manual starting by an upward rather than a horizontal pull.

— Reels of reel-type mower with the maximum number of blades spaced close to each other, giving more cutting per linear foot of forward travel, and therefore doing a better job on the lawn.

— Electric mowers (which have no starting problems) are ideal for the elderly or those with heart conditions. They are light and very effective on small lawns.

— Staggered wheels, to prevent ruts in the lawn.

— A cover, to prevent rust.

— A good range of cutting heights, from ¾ inch to 3 inches (2 to 7.5 cm).
— A fairly narrow mower — say 19 inches (48 cm) for cutting the grass between trees and bushes
— A wide mower for straight up-and-down work — this is obviously quicker.
— A silencer to cut down noise.

Using the mower

Maintenance of the lawn

Frequency of mowing is dictated largely by the type of grass. Grass mixtures containing Kentucky bluegrass should not be cut lower than 1½ inches (4 cm). You should only cut between 1/32 and ¾ inch (0.2 an 2 cm) from a blade of grass. Also, in July and August, you should cut your grass higher — 1½ to 1¾ inch (4 to 4.5 cm) — to protect the crowns against the burning sun.

Grass clippings should be removed every two or three mowings, if your lawn is getting three or four applications of fertilizer during the growth seasons. If the clippings are not removed from lawns where the grass grows strongly, a layer of culm builds up — sometimes more than ¼ inch (0.8 cm) thick — with the result that the roots are stifled. On bluegrass lawns this layer of culm should never be allowed to get more than ¼ inch thick. The culm layer is also a favourite spot for lawn diseases, such as helmintho-spore blight. However, if the lawn is not fertilized at all during the year there is no need to remove the clippings.

Areas shaved bare are the result of too low a cut. If the bare patch has not been 'skinned' too badly, it will usually heal itself in time. However, if there are too many of these bare patches on the same lawn, it generally calls for reseeding.

The first mowing of the spring should be carried out when the grass has grown ½ inch (1.5 cm) above the normal cutting-height. A very common error is to spread fertilizer too early in the spring and thus over-stimulate the grass, which then produces a "plump" growth, full of sap. This means that the lawn must be mown more frequently than normally. If your planned fertilizing programme calls for three or four applications of fertilizer, using the amounts recommended for the growth season, there is no need to carry out the first application before the first or second week of May. Strong applications of fertilizer too early in the season can really harm the grass, since the over-stimulated plants will be adversely affected by the hot weather in July and August.

During the summer holidays, grass is often allowed to grow longer than usual, because the gardener is away on trips and outings far from home. In such cases, do **not** cut the grass back to its normal height at one go. The removal of nearly the whole of the blades of grass, coupled with the fact that the fragile grass-stems have hitherto been protected from the sun, represents a serious shock for the grass-plants. Almost inevitably, they will fade and die. The lawn will take a long time to recover from a mistake like that. Instead, you should lower the height of the cut gradually, removing no more than ¾ inch (2 cm) of grass every two days, until you have got back to the normal cutting-height.

The lawn can be cut to its usual height without any danger until the first snowfall. Letting the grass grow too high during the autumn can be just as harmful as leaving dead leaves on the lawn all through the winter.

There are several reasons why you should not cut grass when it is damp. Apart from the risk of getting your feet wet, it is very hard to get a good cut since the clippings bunch up into balls and if you leave them on the lawn they will stifle the grass. Besides, most pathogenic organisms thrive in damp grass, and freshly-cut areas are wide open to attacks by various diseases. Several micro-organisms can spread to other areas in droplets of water while you are mowing. The best time to mow your lawn is in the afternoon or early evening.

Mowing patterns

On surfaces which are free of obstacles, you should move around the lawn in a clockwise direction. Then mow in the opposite direction, as shown in Sketch #1. This method of mowing will give your lawn a good appearance. The

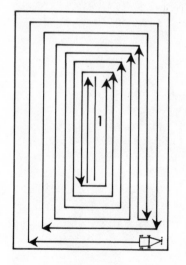 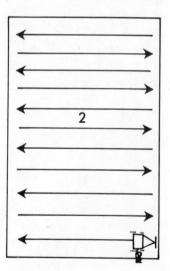

Sketch 1: Mowing pattern for use with motor mowers

Sketch 2: Mowing pattern for use with electric mowers.

use of an electric mower calls for rather more pre-planning — although if your lawn is free of obstacles, it is best to work your way to and fro, moving farther away from the electrical outlet all the time, as you can see in Sketch #2. This is also a good system if the grass is damp or wet. Whenever possible, you should change the pattern every time you mow. If the lawn is always cut in the same direction, the grass will develop a tendency to lie in that direction and will not stand up properly.

Mowing patterns for seated mowers and mini-tractors

This continuous system of mowing, for seated mowers and mini-tractors, does away with 180° turns and time-wasting backing-up. It is advisable to alternate your mowing patterns, to give your lawn a better appearance and to avoid a pattern of wheel-marks. On the left, a diagonal pattern, which follows a triangular path over the ground. On the right, a square or rectangular pattern (to fit the shape of your lawn).

Before you start mowing the lawn, use a pair of clippers to trim the places which the mower cannot reach, such as the edges of flowerbeds and alongside walls, buildings and other obstacles.

Adjusting the height of the cut

Most mowers are equipped with some device which allows adjustment of the height of the cut. On reel-type mowers, the reel itself can be moved up or down. On rotary mowers, the position of the wheels is adjustable, with holes for the axles being provided at different heights. Make sure you use holes at the same level for all four wheels, and screw the nuts on tightly. The most expensive models have an adjusting lever for each wheel. Nearly all mowers are factory-adjusted to give a cut 2 inches (5 cm) high.

Accessories

A collecting-bag for clippings can be attached to most mowers. This accessory plays an important part in the maintenance of the lawn, since it prevents the build-up of culm.

A leaf-sweeper avoids the necessity of having to rake up dead leaves and then burn them. This particular accessory can be fitted to most rotary mowers.

Maintenance of gasoline-driven motors

It is always a good idea to check your tools and equipment before the year's gardening work gets under way. The lawn-mower is the item that is used most often and it therefore merits special attention. First of all, read through

As soon as your new lawn mower is delivered, read the instruction-book carefully and familiarize yourself with the safety precautions

Before you mow the lawn, it is essential to ensure that all children and small domestic animals have been moved away. This simple precaution can avoid a nasty accident.

the instruction manual then carry out a complete maintenance inspection. Check the spark plug, carburettor, filters, motor (especially the condition of the brushes), blades, condition of the wiring and the on-off switch.

All dead grass should be cleared away and any rust-spots cleaned off. Mowers with gasoline-driven motors require more than a surface cleaning. You must free the sprockets, reel or blades from dried grass and leaves. The oil filter in the carburettor should be cleaned or replaced. The spark plug, points, gas-tank and all other parts of the machine must be carefully checked.

This little girl using a rotary motor mower without the supervision of an adult could well hurt herself severely.

Keep your hands and feet well away from the blades when you start the motor of your mower. Wear shoes rather than sandals when you cut the grass. Never forget that the smallest slip may have the most hideous consequences.

Proper maintenance of your mower is extremely important. Small motors can be somewhat temperamental, to say the least, and if they are poorly maintained, starting them will always be a real problem. The carburettor is carefully adjusted at the factory, but it could well need some further adjustment to give the best results. The instruction manual will explain how to go about this. Two-stroke motors frequently turn over roughly at low running speeds but this is nothing to worry about. In the autumn, clean out the exhaust ports and the muffler.

Check the level of the oil in the sump before you start the motor each time you use the machine. Change the oil after every 25 hours of use (once a year, for the average home owner). Keep the cooling-fins of the motor clean, to prevent it from over-heating. Check to see that the blade is firmly attached.

After you have finished mowing, remove all grass from the underside of the mower. Dried grass affects the grass-throwing capacity of the mower and can lead to piles of clippings on the lawn which will spoil its appearance.

Ordinary maintenance of the blade can be carried out with a file. However, if it is really blunt, it should be removed and sharpened on a grindstone or with a file. Make sure you remove the same amount of metal from each side of the blade, otherwise it will vibrate badly as it rotates. If the blade hits a stone and is bent, it must be replaced. Straightening it will weaken it, and it could disintegrate while the machine is in use.

A dirty air-filter reduces the output of any motor. The filter should be cleaned at least twice every season.

The spark plug is a frequent cause of poor starting — either because you have flooded the motor and the plug has become soaked with gasoline, or because it is covered with soot. The spark plug should be cleaned or replaced every spring.

Be very careful with your lawn mower on slopes. You would do better to mow along the slope, rather than up and down — that way, the mower is less likely to run back and cut your feet. Also, you should push the mower rather than pull it.

Motor mower experts advise you never to fill the gas tank while the motor is hot. If you do, you are risking an explosion.

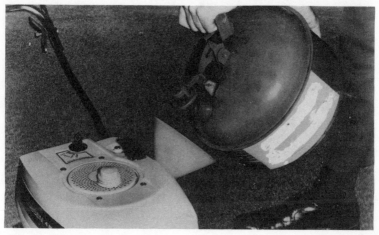

Seated mowers and garden tractors must be driven very carefully along slopes and hills. In such circumstances, cut down your speed and avoid any sudden change of direction or any other quick movement.

One of the first precautions to take when you use motorized lawn-mowing equipment is to wear appropriate clothing. If you catch your sleeve or your trouser-leg in a gear or a moving wheel, you could be very seriously injured

When driving a garden tractor, keep your attention fixed on the job at hand — otherwise it could cost you dearly.

A tractor is not a toy, nor is it meant for joy-rides.

Adjust the slow-running control so that the motor runs fast enough not to keep continually stopping.

For electric mowers, all that is necessary is to inspect the cable to make sure it has not been damaged and to see that all screws are properly tightened. The motor should be oiled occasionally.

Rules to ensure the safe operation of your mower

1. Never put your hands or your feet underneath the mower, or in the grass-discharge vent.
2. Never try to free a blocked discharge vent while the motor is running.
3. Never leave the mower unattended with the motor running.
4. Do not fill the gas-tank of your mower while the motor is still hot.
5. Mow **along** a slope or a bank, not up and down.
6. Never run a gasoline-driven mower inside a garage or any other closed structure.
7. Remove all stones, dog-bones and other rubbish from your lawn before you mow it.
8. Make sure that the blade is securely bolted onto the drive-shaft of the motor.
9. Keep children and pets well away from the mowing area.
10. Never allow chidren to operate lawn-mowers.
11. Do not use electric mowers in the rain.
12. Do not run rotary mowers on gravelly surfaces.

An edge-cutter is the perfect tool for trimming grass along borders, flowerbeds and pathways, and around trees and bushes.

A tractor and a child make a bad combnation. Parents should avoid letting their children use this type of equipment.

Preparing to put the mower away

1. Empty the gasoline from the tank
2. Start the motor and let it run until all the gasoline has gone.
3. Take out the spark plug and put a little oil in the cylinders.
4. Remove any grass that is sticking to the machine.
5. Store the mower in a dry spot.

WATERING AND IRRIGATION EQUIPMENT

When the gardening season begins, remember that grass-plants need a good supply of water if they are to grow normally and keep their beautiful green colour.

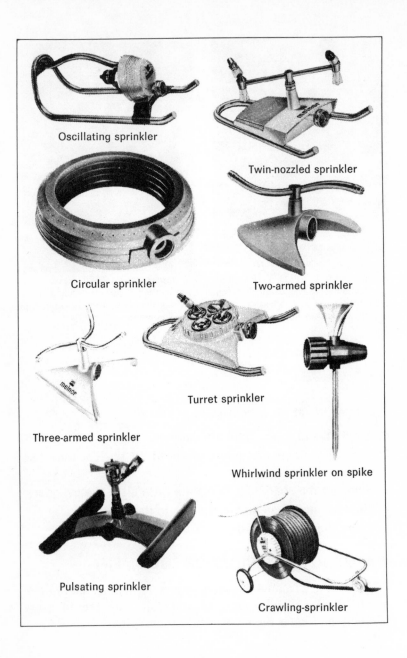

Oscillating sprinkler

Twin-nozzled sprinkler

Circular sprinkler

Two-armed sprinkler

Turret sprinkler

Three-armed sprinkler

Whirlwind sprinkler on spike

Pulsating sprinkler

Crawling-sprinkler

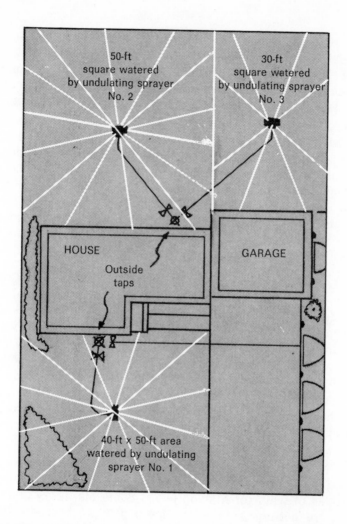

50-ft square watered by undulating sprayer No. 2

30-ft square watered by undulating sprayer No. 3

HOUSE

Outside taps

GARAGE

40-ft x 50-ft area watered by undulating sprayer No. 1

An underground automatic watering system, consisting of three undulating sprayers and five pop-up sprayers, is quite adequate to cover a medium-sized lawn such as the one shown above. This particular installation calls for only four runs of piping To instal such a system, it is quite unnecessary to tear the lawn up, nor do you need to be a plumber or an electrician. An amateur gardener can put the system in quite easily in a few hours.

251

The best results are obtained by watering in the small hours of the morning — i.e., after midnight. At that time there is usually very little wind, evaporation is at a minimum since there is no sun, and water-pressure is at its maximum.

The required lengh of time for watering will vary with the climatic zone. The yardstick is what is known as the "weekly precipitation" — the number of inches of water that are needed every week. Find out from the accredited agent for the equipment how much water your particular installation can supply in one hour, and also how much your lawn needs every week. This latter figure becomes much more important during July, in view of the seasonal rise in temperature. You should then adjust the control mechanism of your system to conform with the demand.

Example If your system can provide 0.35 inch (8mm) per hour and if your climatic zone calls for 1 inch (2.5 cm) of water over and above the weekly rainfall each week to make the grass grow properly, then you should adjust your control mechanism so that each sprinkler works for 50 minutes every second night, or for 25 minutes every night, so that in one week a total of 1 inch (2.5 cm) is delivered.

You should make sure that your sprinkler's capacity and method of operation are suited to the surface area of your lawn. If you already own a sprinkler, you should check that it is working properly at the beginning of spring.

There are a great many different watering systems. A good sprinkler should produce a fine spray, to avoid causing trickles of water or forming pools. Some stationary sprinklers are becoming more and more popular, because they water large lawns without the need for supervision. Crawling sprinklers give uniform coverage of a large surface area. Some models can automatically water tracts of lawn between 30 and 40 feet long (9 to 12 m) in an hour. To water between shrubs and in flowerbeds, many people use canvas irrigators or tubular sprinklers.

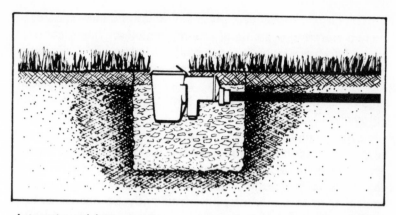

Automatic undulating sprayers cover more ground than the ordinary oscillating sprinkler attached to a hose. The sprayers are installed underground, and are thus never in the way. They can be regulated to cover various areas (squares or rectangles) up to a maximum of 50' x 50'. Each undulating sprayer applies exactly the desired amount of water to ensure a really vigorous growth of grass.

Automatic pop-up sprayers are meant for the hard-to-get-at areas of the lawn, or for watering flowers and bushes. They rise up out of the ground to do their watering, and sink down automatically afterwards. They never get in the way of people walking about on the lawn, nor can they damage your lawnmower.

On large properties, more and more automatic underground watering systems are being installed. These consist essentially of a network of piping buried in the soil, with nozzles at ground level at several places so as to water the whole area of the lawn. Such systems also include regulating mechanisms which turn the water on and off automatically.

With a minimum of care and maintenance these buried nozzles will last for several years, and will help to give a thick, healthy growth of grass. However, it is essential for the user to have a through understanding of how the automatic control mechanism works, how frequently he should water and what method of operation is best suited to the local climate and weekly precipitation, and to the capacity of his system. The photograph shows some of the types of nozzle currently available for underground watering systems.

Whatever the model or models you choose, you must

| Rotating | Undulating | Fixed-jet | All-purpose retractable |

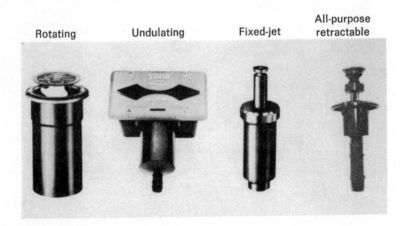

acquaint yourself with how it works, how to regulate it and how to maintain it.

Geared rotating sprayers

How they work

When a geared, rotating sprayer is in operation, it goes slowly round and round, thus distributing water evenly over the surface of the lawn. The watered zone from each sprayer partially overlaps the watered zone from the neighbouring sprayer, and this ensures a uniform distribution of water everywhere. The geared sprayer is ideally suited to every kind of ground. It is, in fact, designed to deliver water in a fairly gentle manner. The water comes down in a fine spray and sinks into the soil. It does not trickle away uselessly and thus there is very little waste. To distribute a larger or a smaller amount of water, all you need do is set the regulating mechanism for a longer or a shorter period of operation.

Regulation

The semi-circular sprayer can be regulated quite easily to cover an arc of 270°. Start by watching the sprayer in action and then decide how it needs to be regulated. Stand behind the sprayer and align the left side of the watering arc along the edge of the area to be covered. This process of alignment can be carried out either by twisting the complete watering-nozzle on its column, or by lifting the mechanism out of its casing and then replacing it in the appropriate position. The area of the watered surface can be altered quite simply with a screwdriver, as follows: Press down the spring knob located below the cap: then (A) to **increase** the watered surface, turn the nozzle clockwise with the screwdriver, keeping the knob pressed down; (B) to **decrease** the surface, turn the nozzle counter-clockwise. As long as the knob is kept pressed down, the nozzle will move in a series of clicks, each click representing 2° of rotation.

Full-circular sprayers cannot be regulated. They distribute water round the full 360° circle.

REGULATING KNOB

INTERIOR VIEW

Maintenance

Naturally, you should clip the grass around the watering-nozzle so that no big tufts are left to deflect or cut down the jet of water. Check at regular intervals.

To increase the area covered

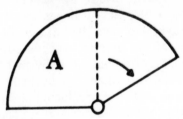

The filter

By removing the screw in the cap, and then the locking-ring, you can pull out the whole drive mechanism in order to clean the filter.

To decrease the area covered

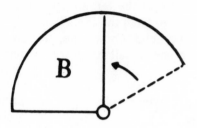

Oscillating sprayers

How they work

This type of sprayer moves back and forth in an arc that can be regulated. It allows for watering of square or rectangular areas up to 45 x 45 ft (13.7 x13.7 m), depending on the water-pressure and the area to be covered. It works very satisfactorily on all types of ground and on all open lawns. The drive mechanism ensures an even distribution of water over grassed surfaces. The sturdy Cycolac casing resists corrosion and stands up well under the weight of foot-traffic and lawn-mowers.

Regulation

1. Regulate the sprayer while it is in operation.
2. Twist the nozzle on its shaft to align the right-hand side of the area to be watered. Move the nozzle **against** the rotation of the shaft, using a screwdriver against the side of the nozzle as a lever.
3. To regulate the left-hand side of the area to be watered, press down on the control flap located on the upper surface of the sprayer. To reduce the angle of arc, press the flap while the head is moving from left to right:

to increase the angle, press it while the head is moving from right to left.

4. To reduce the size of the jet, all you need do is cut down the supply of water from the tap. (This is only valid if there is a tap above-ground. Otherwise, the size of the jet is regulated once and for all when the system is installed).

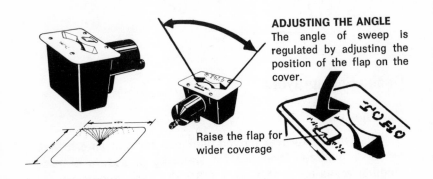

ADJUSTING THE ANGLE
The angle of sweep is regulated by adjusting the position of the flap on the cover.

Raise the flap for wider coverage

Maintenance

As before, you should cut the grass around the sprayer periodically, so that the jet of water is not obstructed by high grass. You should also examine the sprayer-head every now and then and remove any foreign bodies which might interfere with the jet.

Nozzles which have become blocked by limestone scale or other deposits can be cleaned out with a needle or a safety-pin. Remove the cap, then carefully insert a small pin into each of the little holes. Replace the cap and start the sprayer working to flush away the losened scale. Do **not** start the sprayer with the cap off.

NOTE: If there are heavy, whitish deposits of limestone on the nozzle, you may have to remove them by "painting" them with ordinary vinegar until the limestone has been dissolved.

The filter may also be cleaned: just remove the cap and pull the casing out.

Fixed-jet sprayers

How they work

This type of apparatus delivers water in a fixed pattern. The jet covers ¼, ½, ¾, or a full circle, depending on the model. Again, depending on the model, the radius of the spray can be 9, 12 or 15 feet (2.7, 3.6 or 4.5 m). The jet from any one sprayer should partially overlap the jet from the neighbouring sprayer. The nozzle rises up 2 inches (5 cm) when the sprayer is in operation and sinks back to the level of the ground when spraying is finished. Each sprayer-head is provided with a filter designed to prevent obstruction of the flow of water. These filters can be cleaned.

Regulation

Sprayer-heads which cover only part of a circle can be regulated so as to reduce the radius of the spray. This is done very simply, by tightening the screw located in the upper part of the nozzle.

WARNING: Do not reduce the radius by more than 30%, otherwise you may distort the jet of water.

Maintenance

If foreign bodies or deposits have somehow or other found their way into the piping and are obstructing the sprayer, the interior filter should be cleaned. To do this, first turn off the supply of water. Then unscrew and remove the top cap. Take out the column with the filter in it then slip the filter out of the column and flush it through until it is completely clean. Then put everything back in place.

WARNING: When reassembling, make sure that the key of the filter is properly aligned with the slot in the column beneath the cap.

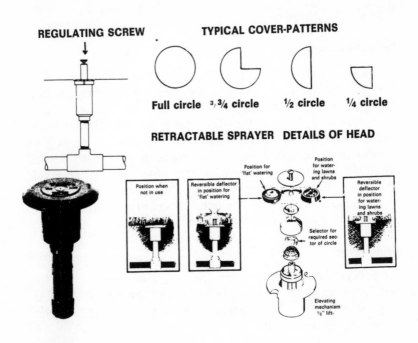

REGULATING SCREW

TYPICAL COVER-PATTERNS

Full circle   3/3/4 circle   1/2 circle   1/4 circle

RETRACTABLE SPRAYER   **DETAILS OF HEAD**

Position when not in use

Reversible deflector in position for 'flat' watering

Position for 'flat' watering

Position for watering lawns and shrubs

Reversible deflector in position for watering lawns and shrubs

Selector for required sector of circle

Elevating mechanism 1/2" lift.

Multiple-nozzle sprayers

Control mechanisms for eleven-nozzle sprayers

These mechanisms contain an electric clock programmed to bring the watering-system into action at the required hour of the day on the required day of the week, the appropriate valves being activated by hydraulic power. By inserting pegs into the two dials, or removing them, it is possible to regulate the system to any desired time-table for a period of two weeks. Once the mechanism has been regulated, the system works automatically throughout the whole watering season. Obviously, if there is a breakdown, the mechanism must be readjusted after the fault has been corrected. It is a good idea to check the 'hour of the day' and the 'day of the week' at regular intervals, to make sure that the regulatory system is working properly.

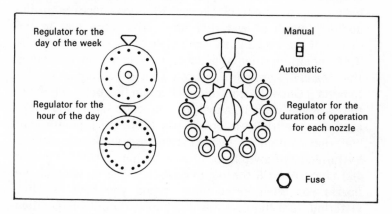

1. Turn the '24 hour' dial clockwise until the actual hour of the day is underneath the arrow. Insert a peg in the '24 hour' dial opposite the hour at which you wish the system to go into action. If you want a second watering during the same day, you must allow a sufficient interval, then place the next peg far enough from the first one to let the system run through its complete cycle. For example, if you have 8 nozzles in service, and each of them is set to water for 30 minutes, then the system will take 8 x 30 = 240 minutes, or 4 hours, to run through a complete cycle. So your pegs must be separated by at least 4 hours' interval — 5 hours would be better.

2. Turn the 'day' dial **counter-clockwise** until the actual day of the week is underneath the arrow. All the holes on this dial should be pegged **except** those for the days on

which you wish the system to operate. (In other words, you must remove the pegs from the holes representing your 'watering' days.)

NOTE: The best time to water lawns is in the early hours of the morning, i.e., after midnight.

3. The control mechanism contains eleven knobs, one for each nozzle. Each knob is calibrated from 0 to 60 minutes: turn each of them clockwise to correspond with the desired length of watering time. The large dial in the centre of the knobs is the 'selector'. This should be in the 'OFF' position when the sprayers are not in operation. The 'Manual/Automatic' switch should be turned to 'Automatic'. Once the control mechanism has been regulated the way you want it, check it over once again and make sure the electricity is on. If you prefer to regulate your watering system by hand, cancel the automatic control by turning the switch to 'Manual', then turn the selector dial clockwise till the pointer reaches the number of the nozzle you wish to activate. When you have finished watering, turn the selector dial back to the 'OFF' position and put the switch back onto 'Automatic'.

NOTES: (1) If you want to miss a day, or even a complete cycle, turn the switch to "Manual" Make sure, however, that the selector dial is properly in the 'OFF' position.

(2) If you own a 'Clientèle' model, you must push your selector dial inward before it can be turned.

Control mechanisms for four-nozzle sprayers

Instructions for these will be found inside the cover.

There are two versions of this mechanism: in the first, all the nozzles function for 30 minutes every day or every other day; in the second, they work for 60 minutes.

The 60-minute mechanism can be regulated to operate four times a day. However, as before, you should allow a period of five hours for each watering-cycle. The 30-minute mechanism can be regualted to operate up to 9 times a day. If the length of each watering is less than the maximum (i.e., less than 30 or 60 minutes, as applicable), the start of the watering period is delayed by the amount of the shortfall in time. For example: If the first station is programmed to operate for only 20 minutes, and there is a peg in the hole representing 2 a.m., the that station will not come into operation until 2.10 a.m. (for the 30-minute model), or 2.40 a.m. (for the 60-minute model). In other words, if a station is programmed to operate for less than the maximum time, then it will remain idle during the early part of the normal maximum period (either 30 or 60 minutes) and only come into operation after the shortfall in time has expired.

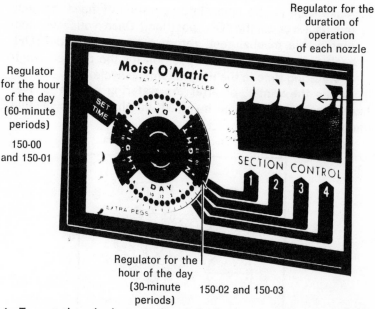

Regulator for the duration of operation of each nozzle

Regulator for the hour of the day (60-minute periods)

150-00 and 150-01

Regulator for the hour of the day (30-minute periods)   150-02 and 150-03

1. To set the clock, turn the dial clockwise until the actual hour of the day is against the large green arrow on the left. You must push inward fairly strongly with your figer-tips against the dial, before it will move.

2. Insert one or more pegs in the dial opposite the hour or hours at which you want the nozzles to start watering. If you want them to operate more than once in 24 hours, you should leave an interval of five hours between the pegs (for the 60-minute model), or three hours (for the 30-minute model).

3. Push down the section control levers numbered 1, 2, 3 and 4, until they are at the number representing your chosen length of watering time. Each click represents about 3 minutes on the 60-minute model, and 1½ minute on the 30-minute model.

4. Check to see that the clock is going, and listen for the sound of the motor running.

5. Make each nozzle come into operation by hand, by pushing its lever to the 'ON' position. Once you have completed this manual test, return the switch to the 'OFF' position, or to the correct position for the desired length of watering time in the next automatic cycle.

During the winter, or after the watering season is over there are several steps involved in shutting down this equipment.

Control mechanism for 11 nozzles

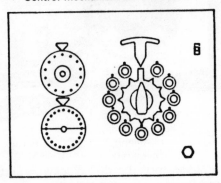

1. Close the main shut-off valve or valves (there may be more than one of them). This valve is likely to be located either near the water-meter or near the automatic valve.

2. Open the drainage valves, which will be either underground or above-ground near the automatic valves. These automatic valves will usually be found on the "sprayer" side of the main shut-off valve. If you are in any doubt as to the location of the various valves, consult the authorized dealer.

3. Set the calibrated knob for each nozzle to '5 minutes'.

4. Turn the selector dial to 'Start', first making sure that the switch is on 'Automatic'. The mechanism will now bring each of the nozzles into action for 5 minutes, thus releasing the pressure in the feed-pipes.

NOTE: Some systems have to be purged by blowing out the pipes with compressed air. Check with the installation crew as to whether this is necessary in your system.

5. Cut off the supply of electricity to the control mechanism.

Control mechanism for 4 nozzles

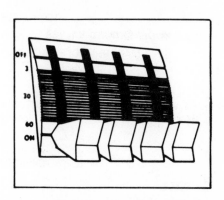

1. Close the main shut-off valve or valves. These may simply be the taps on the flexible above-ground supply hose, or they may be located underground, near the water-meter.

2. Open the drainage valves, which will be either underground or above-ground near the automatic valves. These

latter may be either underground or above-ground, and will usually be on the "sprayer" side of the main shut-off valve. If you are in any doubt as to the location of the various valves, consult the authorized dealer.

3. Push the lever that controls the length of the watering time down to the 'ON' position.

NOTE: Some systems have to be purged by blowing out the pipes with compressed air. Check this point with the installation crew.

4. Cut off the supply of electricity.

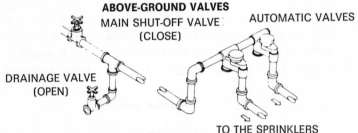

ABOVE-GROUND VALVES
MAIN SHUT-OFF VALVE
(CLOSE)
AUTOMATIC VALVES
DRAINAGE VALVE
(OPEN)
TO THE SPRINKLERS

UNDERGROUND VALVES
MAIN SHUT-OFF VALVE
(CLOSE)
DRAINAGE VALVE
(OPEN)
AUTOMATIC VALVE
TO THE SPRINKLERS

Proceed as follows:

1. Close the main shut-off valve.

2. Open the drainage valves.

3. Cut off the supply of electricity to the control mechanism.

Close the taps on the valve housings and open the exterior taps, to put the valves under pressure.

If you intend to use the exterior tap during the winter for

watering a skating rink, or for any other purpose, disconnect the adaptor coupling, to prevent frost damage within the system.

Starting up again

Control mechanism for
11 nozzles

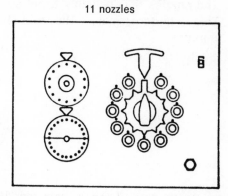

1. Regulate the control mechanism as previously described.
2. Close the drainage valves.
3. Open the main shut-off valve.
4. The nozzle may possibly expel some water immediately. This is quite normal — they will shut down after 15 to 20 minutes.
5. Switch on the electricity.

Control mechanism for
4 nozzles

1. Regulate the control mechanism as previously described.
2. Close the drainage valves.
3. Open the main shut-off valve.
4. The nozzles may possibly expel some water immediately. This is quite normal — They will shut down after 15 to 20 minutes.
5. Switch on the electricity.

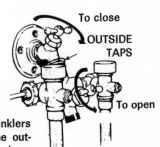

To close

OUTSIDE TAPS

To open

Note Do not worry if one or more sprinklers start working for a few minutes when the outside taps are first turned on by themselves. The sprinklers will stop of their own accord as soon as all the air has been driven from the control pipes.

ABOVE-GROUND VALVES

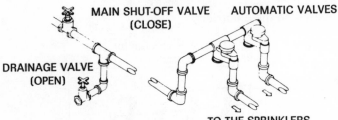

MAIN SHUT-OFF VALVE (CLOSE)

AUTOMATIC VALVES

DRAINAGE VALVE (OPEN)

TO THE SPRINKLERS

Proceed as follows:

1. Close the drainage valves.
2. Open the main shut-off valve.
3. Check that the nozzles and the valves are all in good working order.

4. Test each nozzle for a few minutes to make sure it is working properly.

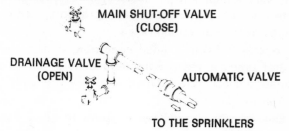

UNDERGROUND VALVES

MAIN SHUT-OFF VALVE
(CLOSE)

DRAINAGE VALVE
(OPEN)

AUTOMATIC VALVE

TO THE SPRINKLERS

Proceed as follows:

1. Close the drainage valves.
2. Open the main shut-off off valve.
3. Check that the nozzles and the valves are all in good working order.
4. Test each nozzle for a few minutes to make sure it is working properly.

Remember to:

1. Regulate the control mechanism.
2. Switch on the electricity.

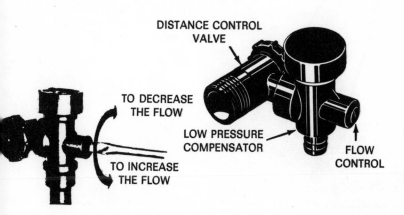

DISTANCE CONTROL
VALVE

TO DECREASE
THE FLOW

TO INCREASE
THE FLOW

LOW PRESSURE
COMPENSATOR

FLOW
CONTROL

Miscellaneous equipment

Apart from the lawn-mower, there is a whole range of tools and equipment to assist you in your task of lawn-maintenance. These include spreaders, edge-trimmers, rollers, lawn aerators and rakes.

To keep a lawn in good condition, it must be fertilized several times a year. **Spreaders** enable you to do this in precise and accurate fashion and they are built to last for several years.

Edge-trimmers and **lawn-clippers** make it easy to trim the grass along borders, walls, buildings, etc.

Lawn aerators let the grass-plants absorb water and nutritive elements more easily.

The lawn-aerator is the ideal instrument for a too closely-packed soil, in which neither water, air, nor nutritive elements can penetrate down to the roots. The piece of equipment shown here is furnished with 8 toothed discs, 10 inches (25 cm) in diameter. It is only 16 inches (40 cm) wide, and is thus suitable for all small lawns.

The all-purpose rake is the perfect tool for removing the culm from the lawn in the spring-time.

Varous types of lawn-clipper

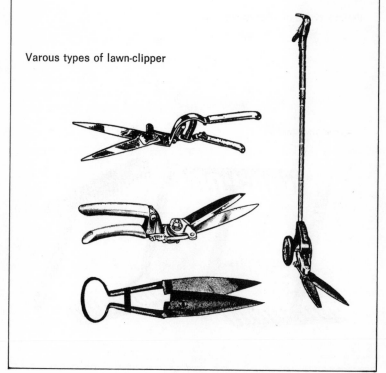

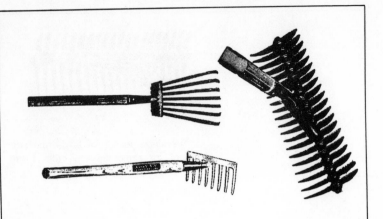

Various types of all-purpose rake

Long-handled rakes

Lawn rollers

Aeration bars for
rollers with rims

The 'gardevator' is a very useful tool for breaking up the soil before sowing seed or laying sod. It is 8 inches (20 cm) wide, has a handle 4 feet (1.2 m) long, and is equipped with 16 steel discs, each with 8 points.

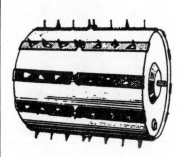

273

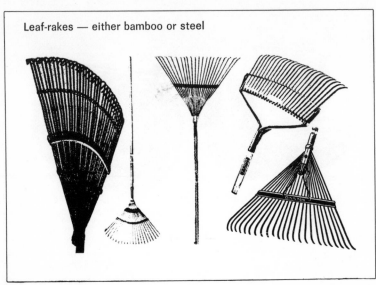

Leaf-rakes — either bamboo or steel

Two very popular models of spreader for fertilizer or seed — the delivery of the contents can be regulated with precision. The one on the left is ideal when you are working at the edge of the lawn near the flowerbeds — it prevents the seeds or fertilizer from being thrown too far. The other spreader is of the 'Cyclone' type and gives uniform coverage over the surface to be treated, saving both time and trouble.

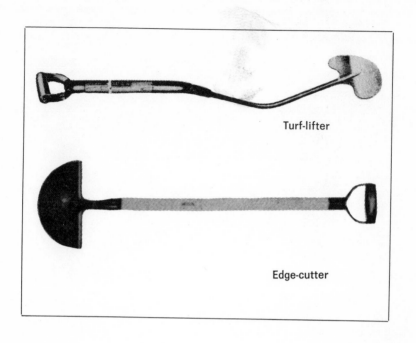

Turf-lifter

Edge-cutter

Printed by
IMPRIMERIE ELECTRA
for
HABITEX BOOKS

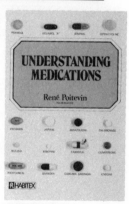

"SOCIAL" DISEASES

A Guide to the Recognition and Treatment of Venereal Disease

Dr. Lionel Gendron

—especially among the young. This book has been written so that the general reader may understand the causes, recognize the symptoms and appreciate the long-term effects of venereal disease.

122 pages,
Fully illustrated

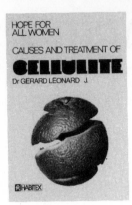

CELLULITE

Dr. Gérard J. Léonard

The author, one of the leading authorities on the subject in Canada, has written a book which will bring hope to all women who suffer from cellulite — hope founded on a scientifically based treatment which has been effective in reducing the problem.

224 pages, Illustrated

WAITING FOR YOUR CHILD

Yvette Pratte-Marchessault

From the first signs of pregnancy to a complete course of postnatal exercises, this straightforward and informative new book provides the answers to the many questions a new mother may ask.

192 pages, Fully illustrated
with photographs and
drawings

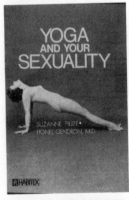

YOGA AND YOUR SEXUALITY

Suzanne Piuze and Lionel Gendron, M.D.

Two well-known authors combine their special knowledge and skills to describe a particular kind of mental and physical harmony — that of mind and sexual function. Physical function is explained, along with the principles of yoga as they apply to a healthy mind and body.

Fully illustrated
190 pages

VISUAL CHESS

Henri Tranquille

This book illustrates simple moves which occur in actual play and which are logical and easy to understand. Many celebrated attacks and defenses drawn from famous games are also included.

175 pages, Illustrated
in two colours

INTERPRETING YOUR DREAMS

Louis Stanké

This fascinating new book, in a dictionary format, will help the reader understand the significance of his dreams and appreciate the activity of his subconscious.

176 pages

TECHNIQUES IN PHOTOGRAPHY

Antoine Desilets,

An invaluable handbook for every one interested in photography — amateur and experienced alike.

262 pages. Fully illustrated with photos, charts and diagrams

TAKING PHOTOGRAPHS

Antoine Desilets in collaboration with Roland Weber

A complete guide to taking photographs, covering such topics as Apparatus, Filters, Film, Light Meters, Flash Lighting, Viewpoint, Portraits and dozens of others.

Fully illustrated 265 pages

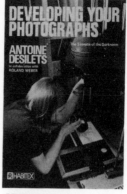

DEVELOPING YOUR PHOTOGRAPHS

Antoine Desilets in collaboration with Roland Weber

Everything you need to know about developing your own films, from choosing basic equipment through enlarging to special effects. A question and answer technique deals with specific questions in detail.

Fully illustrated, colour plates 335 pages

8/SUPER 8/16

André Lafrance

Everything one might want to know about home movies, film making and film production is described in this handbook. It is intended primarily for the amateur, but is also an excellent reference for the more accomplished film-maker.

Illustrated 245 pages

COMPLETE WOODSMAN

Paul Provencher

An invaluable handbook for the serious woodsman, this book is a basic guide to survival in the woods. It contains complete directions for every conceivable situation which might be encountered. A fascinating and useful handbook.

Fully illustrated with line drawings — 225 pages

MUSIC IN QUEBEC 1600-1800

Willy Amtmann

The first survey of musical life in early Canada. It is not a history of music proper, concerning itself with the development of the art, but a cultural history stressing the musical aspects of the story of Canada's early years, of her difficulties, struggles and achievement.

A GUIDE TO SELF-DEFENSE

Louis Arpin

This book is intended for men and women who are not necessarily sportsmen or athletes, but who want to know to defend themselves in an emergency.

304 pages.
Fully illustrated

THE COMPLETE GUIDE TO JUDO

Louis Arpin

Beginning with the origins of the Martial Art known as the Way of Gentleness and proceeding through all the Ground and Standing techniques, this carefully written handbook will be invaluable to anyone interested in the sport.

Fully illustrated
262 pages

SANKUKAI KARATE

Me Yoshinao Nanbu

Karate is a system of defense using no weapons — only feet, knees, elbows, fists, edges of the hands and fingertips. Sankukai karate is a form which uses many techniques developed by the author, Me Yoshinao Nanbu.

Fully illustrated
235 pages

AIKIDO

Text: M. N. di Villadorata
Photos: P. Grisard

Until 1945 Aikido was "reserved" by the elite Japanese military establishment as its special form of self defense. It is a system of attack and defense where one or both participants are armed with staffs, spears, swords or knives.

Fully illustrated
220 pages

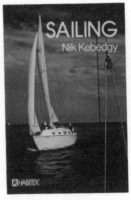

SAILING

Nik Kebedgy

Not just a book for racers, *Sailing* describes some of the background of pleasure sailing and provides much valuable information about the more subtle aspects of the sport.

Fully illustrated
275 pages

GARDENING

Paul Pouliot

Everything the amateur gardener might want to know about gardening in Canada is contained in this outstanding book by a leading Canadian agriculturalist. Topics range from preparing the soil through bulbs, grasses, trees, house plants and plant protection. A Gardening Calendar is a special feature.

Illustrated
465 pages

LIVING IS SELLING

Jean-Marc Chaput

All the tricks of dynamic selling are revealed here by an experienced and successful salesman.

198 pages

CARING FOR YOUR LAWN

Paul Pouliot

The complete guide to the development and maintenance of a beautiful lawn. The author provides many useful tips on lawn care.

Fully illustrated
279 pages

HELP YOURSELF

Psychotherapy Through Reason

Lucien Auger
This guide to self-understanding provides a clear and simple method for overcoming emotional troubles.

168 pages

MOZART SEEN THROUGH 50 MASTERPIECES

Paul Roussel

A fascinating account of Mozart's adult years and the circumstances surrounding the composition of 50 of his greatest works.

344 pages

PHOTO GUIDE

Antoine Desilets

This simple guide provides a handy reference to the basics of still photography.

Fully illustrated
45 pages

SUPER 8 CINE GUIDE

André Lafrance

A technical guide to super 8 photography, designed for use by the amateur as well as the professional.

Fully illustrated
55 pages

A GUIDE TO HOME FREEZING

Suzanne Lapointe

This useful and comprehensive guide to the use of a home freezer is indispensable to anyone who plans ahead. Many ideas, recipes and suggestions are included.

184 pages

A GUIDE TO HOME CANNING

Sister Berthe

An extensive collection of recipes for canning and preserving — ranging from meats and fish through to jams and jellies.

264 pages

BLENDER RECIPES

Juliette Huot

A new collection of recipes and ideas for tasty and nutritious dishes which may be easily prepared using that most versatile kitchen tool — the blender.

174 pages

FEEDING YOUR CHILD

L. Lambert-Lagacé

A useful and valuable guide to preparing nutritious meals for very young children.

245 pages